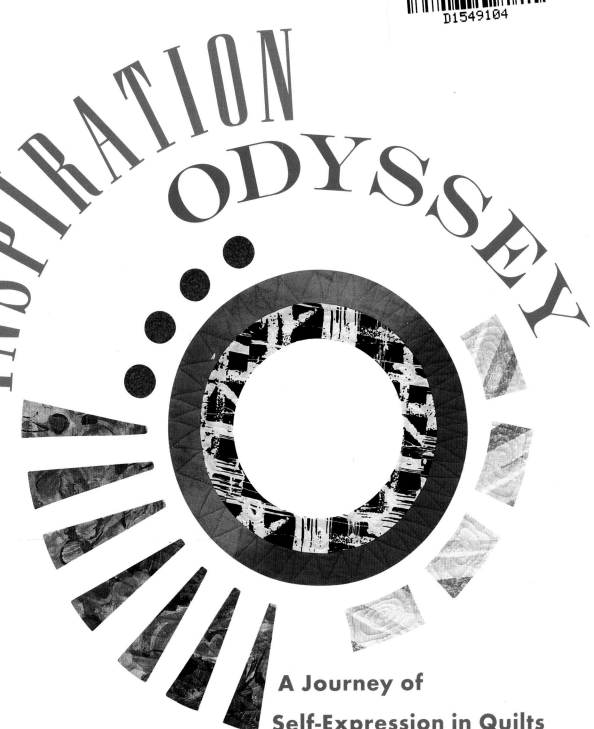

INSPIRATION ODYSSEY

A Journey of Self-Expression in Quilts

**FIBER
STUDIO**
PRESS
An Imprint of
That Patchwork Place

Diana Swim Wessel

FIBER STUDIO PRESS

CREDITS
Editor-in-Chief **Kerry I. Hoffman**
Managing Editor **Judy Petry**
Technical Editor **Janet White**
Copy Editor **Tina Cook**
Proofreader **Melissa Riesland**
Design Director **Kay Green**
Text and Cover Designer **Amy Shayne**
Production Assistant **Claudia L'Heureux**
Illustrator **Bruce Stout**
Photographer **Brent Kane**

MISSION STATEMENT

WE ARE DEDICATED TO PROVIDING QUALITY PRODUCTS AND SERVICES THAT INSPIRE CREATIVITY. WE WORK TOGETHER TO ENRICH THE LIVES WE TOUCH.

That Patchwork Place is a financially responsible ESOP company

Inspiration Odyssey: A Journey of
Self-Expression in Quilts
© 1996 by Diana Swim Wessel
That Patchwork Place, Inc.
PO Box 118
Bothell, WA 98041-0118 USA

Printed in Hong Kong
01 00 99 98 97 96   6 5 4 3 2 1

DEDICATION

This book is dedicated to the children of the world and attempts to capture some of their open, uninhibited approach to art. It is especially dedicated to my five children.

This book has been a journey shared by my entire family. The creative spirit within children is natural and fluid, and I have learned many valuable lessons by watching and listening to mine. They show me that play and free time are important to the creative self. They help me keep everything in perspective, reminding me to stay tuned to the important things in life and let go of the others. I thank my children—Brandt, Ryan, Aaron, Trisha, and Adrian—for inspiring and encouraging my work on this sometimes arduous journey.

ACKNOWLEDGMENTS

My thanks to:

My mother, Jeanette Sciara, who was my first art teacher and will always be a major influence in my life.

My father, William Swim, who encouraged me to seek happiness and take charge of my life.

My brothers, Marc, David, and Jonathan, who have shown me what risk is.

My dear sister, Laura Marie, who has guided me toward the light.

My quilting friends and artist comrades, who supported my first timid steps and provided a link with the art community.

The quilt artists throughout the country who have had a major influence on my quilting journey.

My assistant, Nancy Lewis, who committed huge amounts of time to the completion of this book, despite adverse conditions (working in a house that is also home to five children).

My very talented, longtime best friend, Bonnie Kreckow, a weaver of dreams. She has revealed that we make our dreams a reality.

Library of Congress Cataloging-in-Publication Data
Wessel, Diana Swim,
    Inpiration Odyssey : a journey of self-expression in quilts / Diana Swim Wessel.
        p. cm.
    Includes bibliographical references.
    ISBN 1-56477-168-7
    1. Patchwork. 2. Machine quilting. 3. Quilts —Design. I. Title.
TT835.W484 1996
746.46—dc20   96-22452
                                                                              CIP

TABLE OF
CONTENTS

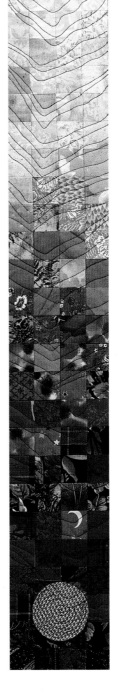

NOTES ON LIFE
AND QUILTS

Art surrounded me in my formative years. With an artist mother, everything got the artist's touch, from a gourmet mushroom pie to a Christmas tree heaped with magically wrapped gifts. My father played a part as well, supporting my mother's creative endeavors and making space for art happenings.

My first experience with fiber was watching my mother embroider. Her embroidery frame was set up in the living room, and the family watched as her stitched pictures came to life. I remember being fascinated by all the different textures and lines she created with needle and yarn.

Hands-on art moved ahead by leaps and bounds when our family moved to a farm in the early 1970s. Batik and tie dye took over the studio, and my mother joined an arts-and-crafts society. We all attended art shows where she displayed her batiked and tie-dyed work. These shows introduced me to a variety of media, giving me the seeds of an art foundation and a wide horizon. When I was college bound, art seemed like the right direction. I majored in interior design at the University of Tennessee at Knoxville.

A 1986 show by the local La Crosse Area Quilters was a major turning point in my life. I was so impressed by the show that I immediately plunged into a quilting life. No longer was I confused. I had a direction to travel, a path to follow. Something inside, my creative spirit, knew that fiber was *it*!

I sought beginning quilting classes and joined the La Crosse Area Quilters group. Sewing with four small children underfoot was almost impossible. Each day was filled with diapers and patches and a lot of late-night stitching. But I had the quilting fever, and I couldn't become a quilter fast enough. Poring over books and magazines, attending quilt-guild meetings and quilt shows, I couldn't wait to learn and explore. Quilting was life, and life was quilting. My quilts gave me a voice, a focus, and the strength to tackle other areas of my life.

Now, nine years into my quilting life—half of which has been spent exploring in my own directions—the medium is even more intriguing. The fiber surface has just been scratched, and possibilities abound. The quilting fever still rages through me.

HOW TO USE
THIS BOOK

This book is for quilters of all levels. Start at the beginning and move through all the sections, step by step, or use it like a road map. As long as you know where you are, you can take off in any direction.

If you want to start at the beginning and follow my process, "Hunting and Gathering" on pages 6–11 will show you where to look for inspiration. If your creative spirit needs stimulation, learn how to translate your inspirations into design drawings with "Design Basics" and "Color Basics" on pages 12–20 and the sketchbook exercises on pages 31–35. If you are confident, have a backlog of ideas, and want to learn methods, go straight to "Construction Techniques" and "Machine Appliqué"on pages 41–46.

The "Design Library" on pages 21–30 includes samples of the raw materials I've used to translate inspiration into fabric: silhouettes to use as base designs, shapes to add interesting detail, quilting lines to emphasize and enhance other design elements.

"Drawing with the Machine" on pages 47–52 explains the techniques I use to draw with my sewing machine. Learn to make a Doodle Sandwich so you can experiment with machine stitching and threads. Each of the exercises in "Fabric Exercises" on pages 58–90 can take you from beginning to advanced levels of skill and complexity. You determine the pace and techniques. I hope my ideas stimulate yours; allow your imagination free rein.

HUNTING
AND GATHERING

The exercises in this section focus on increasing your design awareness and show you how, when, and where to look for designs, images, and patterns for inspiration. As you observe your surroundings more carefully, recording images will come naturally. Gather designs to file away for future use. Have fun in your search. Remember that this is an ongoing expedition. Using this hunting-and-gathering process, you will find your way to personal expression armed with volumes of ideas.

Take small sketch pads and place them in your car and in your bag or purse. Keep paper by you at all times so you can do a quick sketch to capture an idea or outline. You will forget unless you take the time to jot it down.

Keep a scrapbook—your source book—which can be a binder with paper and pocket dividers, to hold your loose findings. Staple or glue tags, paper, note cards, almost anything into this binder. Then you can easily reference your great design inspirations and pore over them for ideas. Label each image, where it came from, when you found it, and why you chose to keep it.

If I have gathered a design that I plan to use soon, I keep it on my bulletin board for easy reference. Placing the design in view keeps my mind churning. My bulletin board is often overflowing with ideas, and designs are taped all over my walls. This method looks untidy, but I need the visual stimulation. I also like to be surrounded by my fabrics, so I store them on open shelves in baskets where I can mix and match with a turn of the head.

1	2	3	4
5	6	7	8
9	10	11	12
13	14	15	16
17	18	19	20
21	22	23	24
25	26	27	28
29	30	31	32
33	34	35	36

1. Paper doily
2. Heraldry
3. Back of clothing label
4. Stamp
5. Newspaper photo
6. Stationery
7. Map
8. Clothing label
9. Silkscreen design
10. Rubbing
11. Wallpaper
12. Magazine ad
13. Bookmark
14. Greeting card
15. Calendar
16. Photo of footprints
17. Greeting card
18. American-Indian art
19. Magazine cover
20. Clothing hang tag
21. Inside of envelope
22. Greeting card
23. Children's book
24. Nintendo® book
25. Children's art
26. Stained glass
27. Greeting card
28. Sale ad
29. Magazine ad
30. Church bulletin
31. Photo of flower
32. Church bulletin
33. Sale ad
34. Magazine ad
35. Pencil packaging
36. Greeting card

Inspiration Sheet

Silhouettes developed from Inspiration Sheet

UNDERWALK

Take a slow walk. The slower you go, the more you see. Look for intriguing patterns and designs on the undersides of objects: leaves, stones, flower petals, bark, insects, butterflies, moths. Keep an open mind. Be fearless in your search. Soles of tennis shoes provide an interesting array of patterns and lines. Look under your carpet (not at the dirt); notice the grid on the back side. Look closer. What do the lines actually look like? I have three carpets and each has a different grid.

Look for the unusual: lines, shapes, clusters of forms, arrangements of color. Every thing is different. Learn to notice the differences. This is an ongoing process that will get easier as you go.

TOMBSTONES

Graveyard symbols offer an unusual set of motifs. Make simple drawings of the stones, and do rubbings of low-relief sculpture. Take plenty of paper—these motifs are large. You can also find a fascinating variety of lettering styles. I have made rubbings of my ancestors' tombstones and plan to incorporate them into a quilt series for a show.

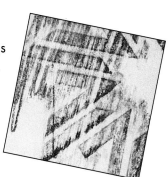

COUNTRY TRIP

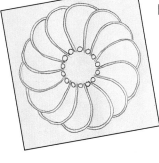

On your next outing, pay attention to the changing landscape, flora, and fauna. Notice the color palettes of the grasses, shrubs, and trees along the roads. Earth and rocky outcrops have different hues in different parts of the country. Oklahoma's red mud is quite a contrast to western Wisconsin's rich black fields.

While long road trips are wonderful, you don't need to travel far. The farms in my area provided me with a marvelous quilting design inspired by a hay rake. Farm machinery, outbuildings, barn roofs, and silos have intriguing angles and textures.

CITY TRIP

Observe the colors, angles, and architectural details of a city. Study the lines of high-rises—the huge glass surfaces reflect many intriguing shapes. At dusk, the lines of the city soften and shadows deepen. At night, buildings glow with the reflected radiance of street lights. On rainy nights, reflections sparkle and run together.

BOUQUETS

You can buy (or hint that someone give you) a bouquet of fresh flowers (silk won't do). Watch the color transformation as the petals dry. Study the metamorphosis, the softening and darkening of the petals and leaves. Turn the petals over and examine the undersides. Invest in a quality set of colored pencils and document the changes.

THE LIBRARY

Every shelf of the library has something to offer; there is an abundance of beautiful books with mouth-watering photographs. Take a viewfinder (page 33) and sketchbook to the library; or don't, and just expand your visual memory.

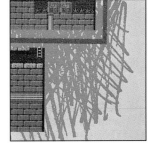

Children's books are excellent sources of unusual and bright color palettes and abstract or whimsical landscapes. They can provide exciting compositions rich with detail and color or with simplified shapes and forms. Children's activity books often include a variety of lines, patterns, and spatial compositions. Video games and game books offer small vignettes—angular scenes that can be enlarged and adapted for quilt designs.

Study books of different artists' work and note the colors and values in their paintings. Look in books of heraldry for coats of arms. Badges, emblems, and symbols can all give you ideas for interpretation. Books about Art Nouveau and Art Deco are excellent catalogs of line and image. Deco compositions are geometric and angular, Nouveau is more organic, with stylized floral motifs, flowing lines, and curved shapes.

Graphic-art books provide excellent illustrations and line drawings that will stimulate your creativity. Architecture books offer geometric forms, angles, and lines adaptable to fabric translation. Books about flags show the basic rectangle divided into colors and geometric shapes.

I remember the wonderful line drawings in my college botany book, which influenced me in my silk-screen design class. Try wildlife magazines for outlines and color combinations. Don't worry about making a realistic sketch. Draw the basic shape (outline), adding only enough detail to capture the idea.

Take a second look at ads in magazines, flyers, and newspapers. Often, overlapping images and colors create special effects. Scan newspapers and newsletters for line drawings that suggest texture. Add those textures to your sketchbook.

Collect motifs, symbols, and shapes with a theme in mind. Many of my celestial designs were inspired by books about the universe.

PHOTOGRAPHY

Use your camera to capture intriguing landscapes, cityscapes, and skyscapes. The camera can isolate images, focusing and framing design options. Translate these into sketches.

WALLPAPER AND FLOOR-COVERING STORES

Go to stores that carry tiles, linoleum, and carpets, keeping your eye and mind open for composition study. Why do you like or dislike a particular pattern? How would you use fabric to re-create these textures? For example, glazed chintz looks like shiny tiles, and flannel has the fuzziness of carpet.

Wallpaper books will overwhelm you with pattern, color, and style. Check them out and bring all those sizzling patterns home, but don't overdo it. Check out only a couple books at a time. Mark your favorite patterns, then review them to decide which ones are worthy to take up a page in your sketchbook. Use colored pencils to capture the colors of the designs, or staple swatches in a scrapbook for future reference.

STAINED-GLASS WINDOWS

Take time to visit churches and look at window designs. Books on contemporary glass designers offer another "window" of opportunity.

LOGOS

Study logos on signs and billboards. You can hardly avoid these images; they are everywhere! Take logos back to your drawing board, and let your imagination reinvent them. Developing an inventory of your own compositions will become easier as you train your eye to see.

NAPKINS, DOILIES, PAPER TOWELS, AND STATIONERY

Ask yourself what makes the pattern or design on each item successful. Study borders, embossing, overlapping shapes, and line. Collect items that have strong graphic images and outlines.

FASHION STUDY

Clothing can be an excellent source of unusual color and pattern. It doesn't have to be high fashion. Pay attention to details: collars, cuffs, front plackets, and yokes.

CLOTHING TAGS AND LABELS

Clothing tags offer intriguing miniscapes. Observe the division of space, pattern, scale, and color.

DISHES (EVEN THE DIRTY ONES)

The borders on plates offer a variety of motifs and floral images. Investigate over, under, and inside. My son Ryan's dried cocoa-cup remains presented an intriguing arrangement of lines.

CHILDREN'S ARTWORK

We have a steady stream (a flood, actually) of wonderful art coming into our home from four school-age children. Children use color with abandon, sometimes combining hues in unexpected and jolting ways. Their drawings are kid perspectives and offer interesting displays of shape and color. Kid perspective can enlighten any viewer with fresh images and patterns. Children express their emotions directly on the canvas. Try to feel the emotions when you study children's art.

FROZEN ENVIRONMENT

In winter, if you are lucky enough (ha!) to have snow and cold, you can find designs. Frost on windows presents a random pattern of line. My son once tracked in snow on our gray kitchen carpet. I stooped to pick it up and looked close. There was a partial imprint, a snow casting, of the soles of his tennis shoes. The lines of his shoes in the white snow against the gray textured carpet revealed an instant, successful design.

STAMPS AND STAMP-COLLECTING BOOKS

Be sure to check all your incoming mail.

LITURGICAL CLOTHS

Banners and robes provide a variety of simplified motifs and abstracted shapes. Dramatic color use, bold contrast, and intense hues represent and evoke certain moods.

MIRROR PLAY

Walk, sit, or lie down with a 12" x 18" (or smaller) mirror. One without a frame works best. Look in the mirror. Study the angles, perspectives, and repeats in the images you see.

Set the mirror by a patterned surface, tilt it at different angles, and watch the patterns change. Symmetrical images appear in the reflections. Hold the mirror flat, facing the ceiling, and study the reflected shapes to gain a new perspective. Take the mirror outside. Watch the world turn upside down, but be careful. You may feel as though you are the one turning upside down.

DESIGN BASICS

TOOLS

Colored pencils, to create a color plan.

Oil pastels, for color play.

Viewfinders, to gather silhouettes.

Bulletin board, to display your ideas while working.

Compass, for designing curves.

Ruler, for measuring and drawing straight lines.

Kaleidoscope with clear prisms, to fracture your world.

Paint chips, for visualizing color choices.

One three-year-old, who is upside down most of the time, definitely provides a unique perspective.

Graph paper, for drawing designs. Graph paper is available in different-size grids. You can also reduce and enlarge the grids on a copy machine for more design flexibility. Experiment with cutting apart the grids and reassembling them into new configurations.

Sketchbooks, to practice, practice, practice sketching. I have one large sketchbook and many smaller pads. I keep them in several places: by the bed, in my purse, in the car, and by the telephone. At night, when you have an idea flash, quickly make note of it before the image fades into oblivion.

Three-ring binder with pocket dividers, for storing sketches and other images. Sometimes I staple small sketches to a larger piece of paper for easier viewing and note making. Keep in mind this is your personal collection. It doesn't have to be finished, polished, or slick.

ELEMENTS OF DESIGN

Learning basic design elements will help you create a dynamic silhouette (base design). These concepts will guide your arrangement of shapes, lines, and colors for a pleasing balance. Keep in mind that the elements of design are not separate, compartment-like concepts. Each overlaps and intertwines to produce a mesh of visual factors. Look around you to see how these principles occur in nature and how they have been used by man. As you look at designs, try to see how artists use these techniques to create visual harmony.

Familiarize yourself with the basic design elements; they will guide your work toward order and harmony. Once you know the rules, you can confidently break them to express your individuality.

UNITY

Unity is a condition of harmony within a composition. Unity gives you the sense that the elements of the design belong together and are related. This can be accomplished most obviously and easily by repeating shapes, colors, lines, textures, or patterns. You can also achieve unity by placing elements close to one another, or by placing them in a connected or continuous arrangement.

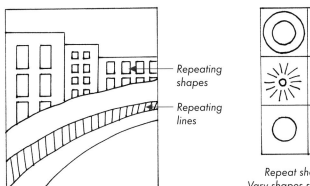

Repeating shapes

Repeating lines

Repeat shapes to create unity.
Vary shapes slightly to create interest.

BALANCE

Symmetrical designs and designs with an equal balance of shapes create unity through repetition, as in "Reflection" on page 78. Balance can also be achieved by repeating color, value, or texture within the composition. Symmetrical balance is orderly, calm, and predictable.

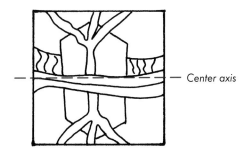

Center axis

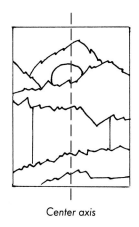

Center axis

Asymmetrical design can be balanced or not. Balancing an asymmetrical composition requires you to equalize the visual importance of the two sides so the eye is pleased and calmed by the overall effect.

Imbalance and unequal distribution of shapes is dynamic, since the eye is drawn from one area to the other. The most pleasing design often occurs when you divide space unequally. Imbalance evokes tension and intrigue, as in "Fires Above" and "Night Fire" on page 81.

Try using a simple rule of thirds. Divide your space into three areas, either vertically, horizontally, or medallion style (center out), as shown in "Sunrise Windows" on page 67 and "Reign of the Sun" on page 76. Or divide space by repeating geometric shapes to create a simplified silhouette.

Rule of Thirds

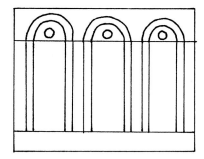

Space divided vertically.

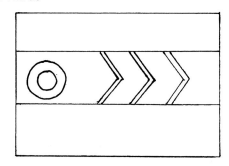

Space divided horizontally.

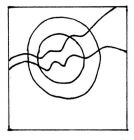
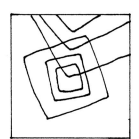
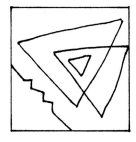

Shape is the most powerful repeating element. Try dividing space with one of three shapes: circle, square, or triangle.

FOCAL POINT

The focal point of a design is the place where the eye naturally comes to rest. Detail, color, or line can direct the eye toward the focal point. A small, detailed shape—what I call a "design window"—can create a focal point. Balanced by a much larger, less detailed space, it draws the viewer in.

Develop a design window by creating a detailed miniature design. Place this window on a background that echoes the colors, lines, and shapes in the design window. Repeating shapes on a larger scale creates unity. See "Night of the Moon" on page 88. Practice making a design window on paper. Experimenting with paper gives you the freedom to express many ideas and choose your favorites to translate into fabric.

Balance and emphasize your focal point by placing it within a frame. See "I Want the Window" on page 66 and "Windmill Wash" on page 62.

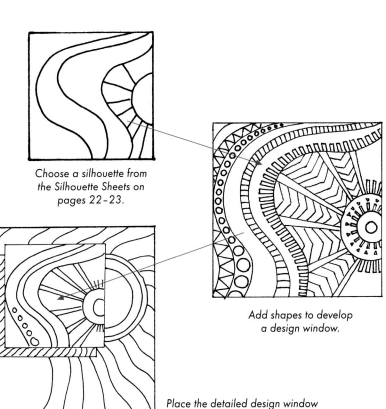

Choose a silhouette from the Silhouette Sheets on pages 22-23.

Add shapes to develop a design window.

Place the detailed design window on a less detailed background to create a focal point.

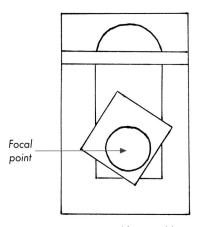

Focal point

Foreground frame adds depth to composition.

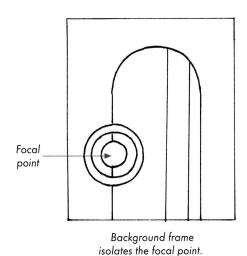

Focal point

Background frame isolates the focal point.

SCALE AND SHAPE

Varying the scale of the shapes in a design creates a more dynamic composition. Repeating a shape establishes unity. Combine the two concepts by repeating a shape in different scales for unity with variety.

Cut out simple paper shapes and play with arrangements. Practice in your sketchbook, creating simple geometric silhouettes. Work quickly to generate as many ideas as possible. This is brainstorming time, part of the process that starts the creative flow. It might take you twenty pages to come up with one workable plan, and that's OK. Practice working in your sketchbook, becoming familiar and comfortable with translating ideas to paper. See "Night Pages" on page 71 and "Night Moons" on page 72, quilts with strong repeating elements.

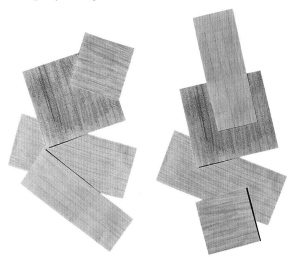

Play with arrangements of shapes.

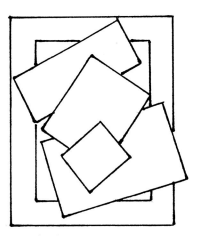

Sketch an arrangement to create a design.

Color. Just speaking the word brings chilling, paralyzing fear into the hearts of some quilters. Have you ever stalled on a project when it came to choosing colors? In this section, we will explore some ways to demystify the color-selection process.

Color preference is subjective. As with music and dance, everyone has individual tastes. If you study any of the nationally recognized quilt artists, each has not only a highly recognizable style, but also a definite color personality.

Increasing your awareness of color through observation is the beginning of boosting your confidence. By viewing a wide variety of color schemes, you can refine and nurture your color sense. This ongoing exploration will help you develop your color personality. Exploring unfamiliar territory keeps your ideas fresh, preventing boredom from setting in. With practice, exploring unique color combinations will be less intimidating and actually become one of the extremely exciting aspects of design.

QUALITIES OF COLOR

A **hue** is a color. The primary colors are yellow, red, and blue. All other colors can be mixed from these three.

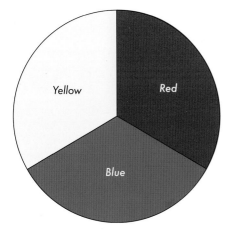

Primary Colors

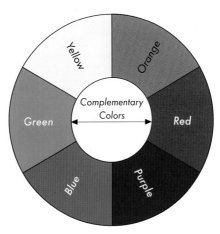

*Secondary Colors:
Orange, green, and purple*

Value is the degree of lightness or darkness of a color. A lighter value, or tint, is made by adding white to a hue. A darker value, or shade, is made by adding black to a hue. The apparent degree of lightness or darkness of a hue is affected by adjacent values. The normal human eye is capable of differentiating 100 steps from black to white.

Saturation is the degree of intensity of a hue; a full-strength color (no white, black, or other color added) is said to be saturated.

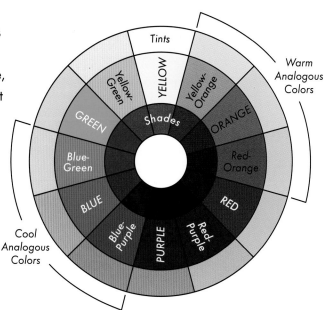

COLOR PALETTES

The color palette is the range of colors you choose for a particular design. The most frequently used color compositions are complementary and analogous. **Complementary** colors lie opposite each other on the color wheel. For example, blue and orange are complementary colors. When complementary colors are placed next to each other, they intensify each other. Many modern artists juxtapose complementary colors to stimulate a strong reaction.

Analogous colors are adjacent to each other on the color wheel. They blend and harmonize.

Do not count white, gray, or black as colors when choosing a palette or scheme for your design. These are neutrals.

Complementary Color Study - Subdued compliments
9.95

Complementary Color Study - Warm and Cool Combinations
9.95

Neutrals bring unity to divergent hues and provide an effective background for brilliant hues.

Avoid over-coordinating and over-blending print fabrics. Add a bit of a discordant hue to generate the spark or tension that holds interest. Learn from the wonderful, sometimes odd combinations of hues in antique scrap quilts.

Analogous Color Harmony   10-95

A dizzying selection of hues is available in fabric stores. Dyeing your own fabrics opens the door to even more choices. Color wheels serve as guides and reminders of the spectrum of colors available, but you must experiment and explore color relationships to develop your unique color sense.

Color can accentuate design elements or make selected areas blend. Strong color can direct the eye toward a focal point. Warm colors advance and cool colors recede. Squint at "Windmill Wash" on page 62. Which areas come forward and which seem to sink away?

Cool

Warm

COLOR MOOD

Color is a very personal, expressive choice. You can use a color palette to evoke a certain mood or feeling. Each of us has a predominant color mood. Look at your wardrobe (past the denim jeans) to find out what colors you gravitate to and what color personality you portray.

Each color has strong characteristics. Our reactions to a color vary depending on the color's intensity, value, and temperature. Red, a warm color, provokes intense feelings: anger, passion, even aggressiveness. Sherbet colors suggest springlike cheerfulness. Black is somber. Blues and greens are cool; they promote calm and serenity. Color projects a powerful message.

COLOR STUDIES

Use the exercises in this section to explore color. They will help you select workable palettes for your designs.

MOOD STUDY

Build a color palette from a distinctive, multicolored fabric. Build around the mood of the main swatch, choosing complementary prints, solids, and textures.

Choose a swatch from the Color Composition Sheets on pages 29–30. Each square contains enough colors to produce a full palette. Choose one fabric swatch from the sheet and identify the hues in the fabric. Try to find fabrics in light to dark values of each hue in the swatch. This process will develop your color sense.

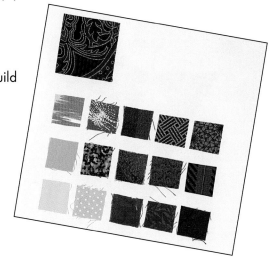

COLOR-STRIP STUDY

Look for fabrics that have a color strip on the selvage. This strip shows the dyes used to print the fabric. Use the color strip as a palette. Select fabrics in a range of values, in the colors shown on the strip.

FASHION STUDY

Look at clothing with colors you find fascinating. Fashion designers are experts at successfully combining colors. Follow their lead. Patterned socks turned inside out provide a wonderful tangle of lines and hues. Study the color combinations and relationships. Pull out hues, then add darks and lights to create a palette. Record these in your sketchbook.

ENVIRONMENT STUDY

Examine the urban environment: the interiors and exteriors of homes, offices, and retail establishments, and signs, billboards, and roads (gravel and pavement). Automobiles often sport unusual hues. Watch the road, and be aware.

Observe nature, flowers, insects, fish. See the myriad hues, and record them in your sketchbook. Take your sketchbook and colored pencils outside to re-create natural colors in natural light. Use your camera as a tool to capture color.

Close examination of nature shows us that leaves exhibit a variety of hues, as do other natural objects—rocks, earth, and such. These appear to us as flat planes of color, but are actually composed of complementary hues with neutrals to bring harmony.

Look closely at the objects you find. In my sketchbook study of wilted lilac petals and leaves, I first sketched the shapes, then concentrated on color. Try to capture subtle shadings. After close examination, you will notice a range of colors you can use as a color palette. Try to identify the intense accent color that is usually present.

DESIGN
LIBRARY

This section contains reference sheets from which you can select design elements for your experiments. Eventually, you will collect a library of your own design elements.

Silhouette Sheets: I use the term "silhouette" to describe a line drawing, a simple division of space I use as my design building block, a base design. I use viewfinders to discover silhouettes. The silhouette, or base design, can be developed further by subdividing spaces and adding shapes. The base designs on page 28 are from some of the quilts in this book.

Shape Sheets: A wide variety of shapes, from simple to complex. Add them to a silhouette to elaborate the design.

Line Lingo: Samples of quilting patterns to stimulate and guide you in developing a quilting diagram. A quilting diagram is a road map of the quilting lines you intend to stitch on your quilt. A variety of lines adds excitement to a design.

Color Composition Sheets: A wide range of multicolored swatches. Each square can be developed into a color palette (color scheme).

Silhouette Sheet

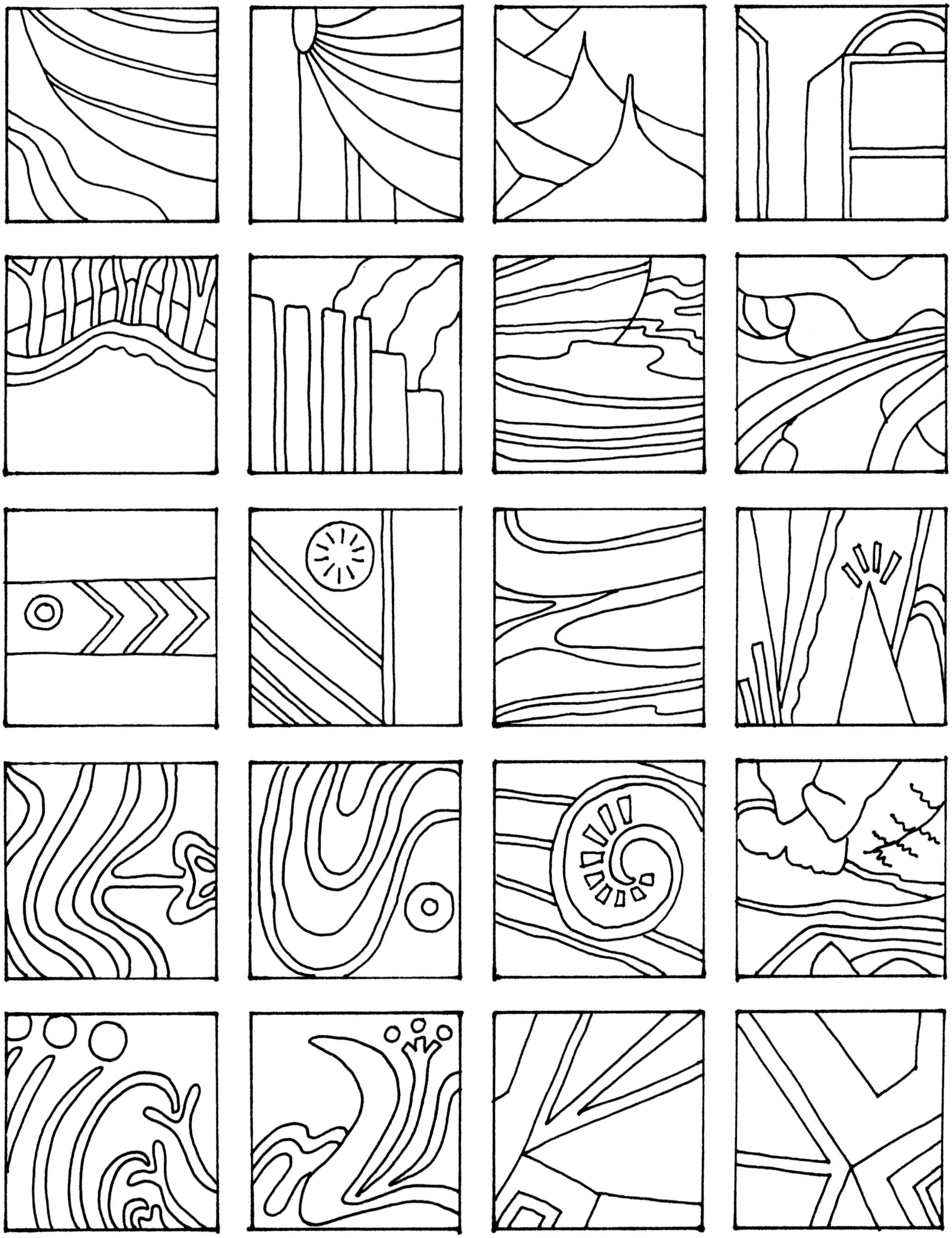

Shape Sheet

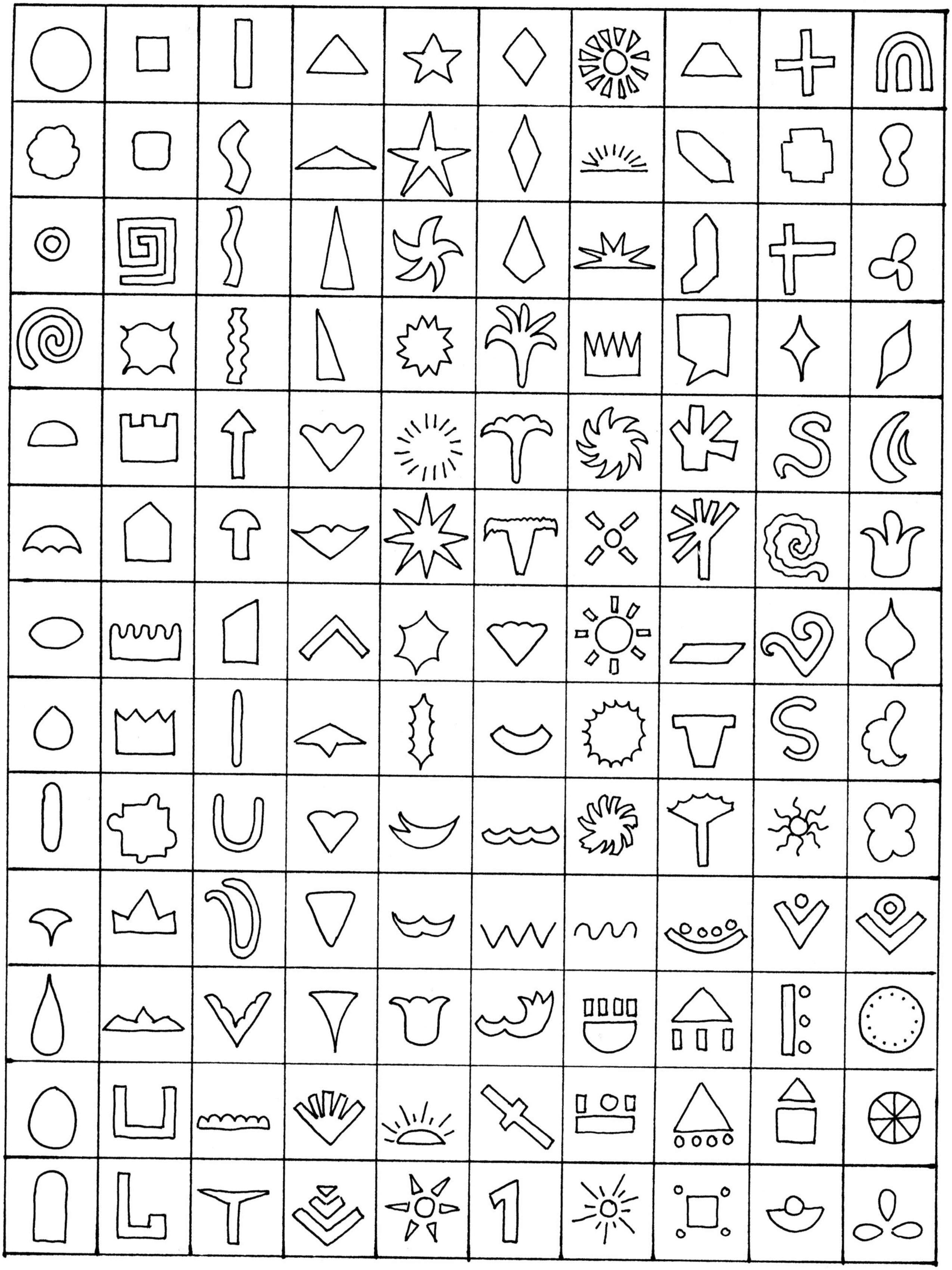

Shape Sheet

25

Line Lingo

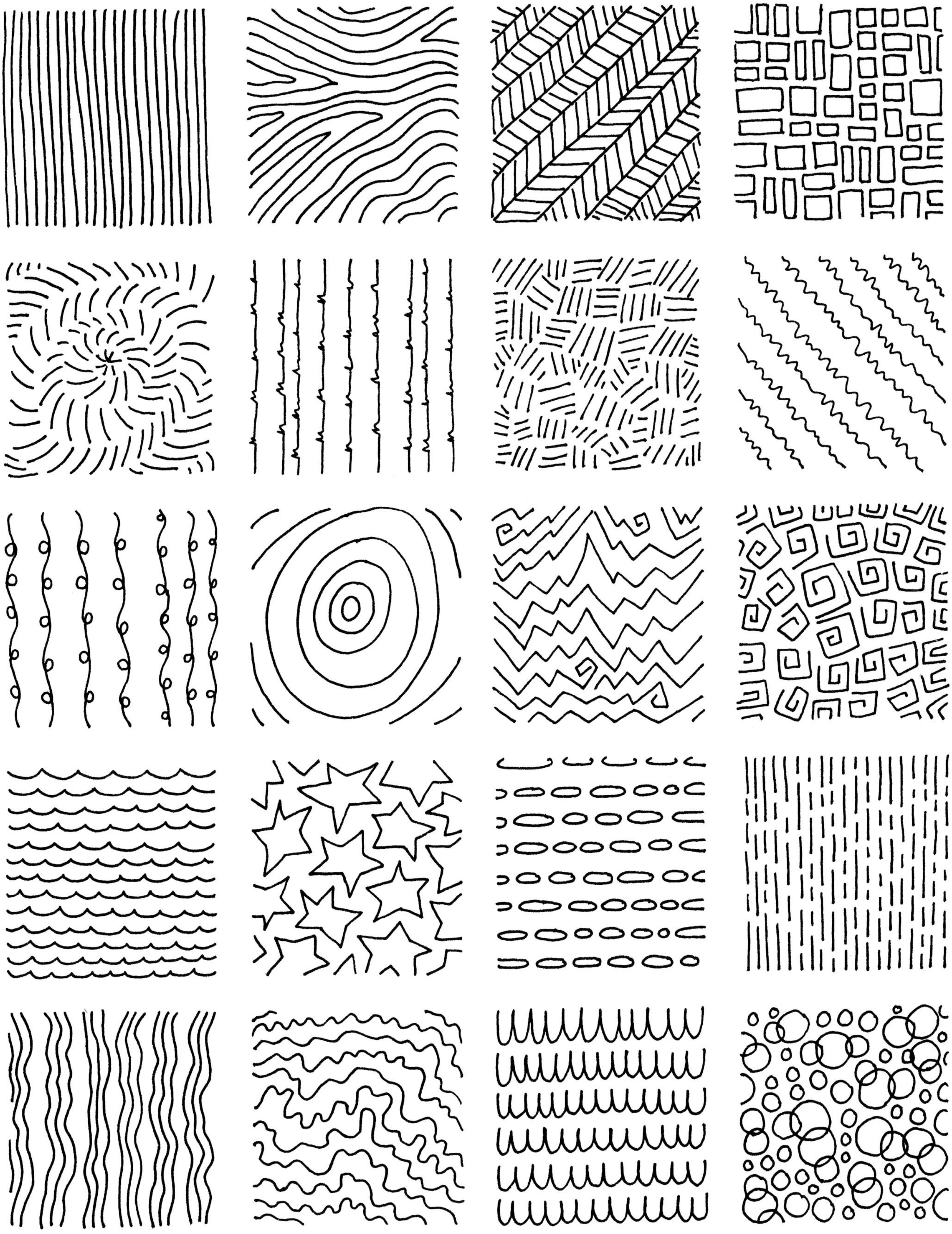

Silhouette Sheet

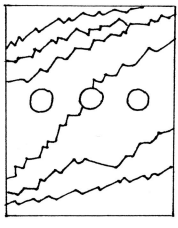

"Heat of the Star"

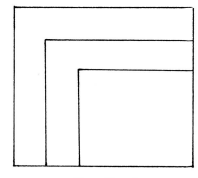

"Night Pages"

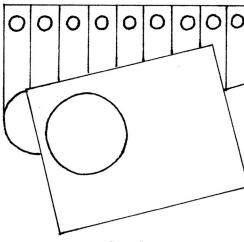

"Vistas"

"Fires Above"

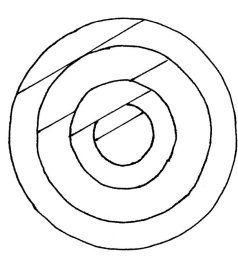

"Night of the Moon"

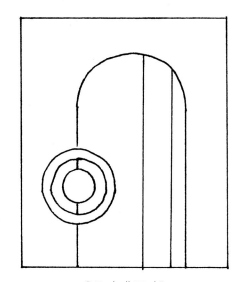

"Windmill Wash"

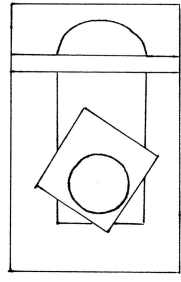

"I Want the Window"

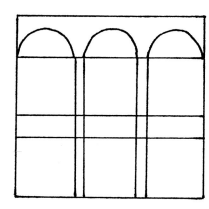

"River's Edge"

28

29

Color Composition Sheet

30

SKETCHBOOK STUDIES

Exploring and observing, you will be surprised at the creative power within you. Learning to tap into this artistic spirit is an ongoing effort. To depart from tried and true methods and comfortable color combinations, to boldly go where no quilter has gone before, is part of the creative journey.

My two-year-old son drew on paper, but soon made a departure from the usual and explored drawing on the table. As fiber artists, we must depart from the usual, exploring every possible direction and releasing our creative spirits. We must keep our minds open, letting go of all the "must do" rules. There are many paths to walk, many right ways.

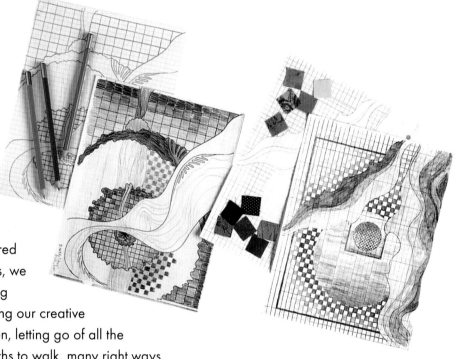

This sketchbook section will help you increase your understanding of design through sketching. In a line drawing, line alone produces form, a silhouette. Using line without color allows us to concentrate on dividing space and developing a composition.

Work on paper with your design, quilting diagrams, and color plans. Transferring images to paper often starts a flood of ideas. If a new thought flows through, stop and capture it, whether in words or as a sketch. You can always go back and develop the seed idea further. Just make sure to get it down on paper. When I first began sketching, I did not feel proficient at transferring to paper all the ideas that flashed through my head. I started by playing with color on graph paper. An established grid gave me confidence to start breaking up spaces with lines and shapes. Use graph paper to help guide your lines when you sketch. Store all your small sketches in a scrapbook. I use three-ring binders with pocket folders. Use your binder scrapbook to store found objects that contain or suggest images you want to develop.

From time to time, flip through your scrapbook and sketchbook. Examine all your special findings and sketches. You will be fascinated to see your skills and thoughts growing and changing. Each idea you gather is a seed that can grow into a fully developed piece of work or even a series of works. Use your sketchbook to develop your seed ideas. Try one or all of the following exercises. Each has the potential to set you on a creative path. Feel free to make a departure anywhere your artistic vision reveals another way.

SERIES

Take a thematic approach. Gather images that reflect a central idea. Record these images in your sketchbook. Build several compositions around the images. Out of the many paper quilts you design, take a few you feel are worthy of further exploration in fabric. Working on one design will spark other ideas and start a chain reaction. The quilts "Heat of the Star," "Night Fire," and "Fires Above" on pages 80–81 were developed with a celestial theme.

A small format allows you to try an abundance of designs and produce a series of quilts without making the investment of time and money larger quilts require. The more ideas you work through, the more your confidence will grow.

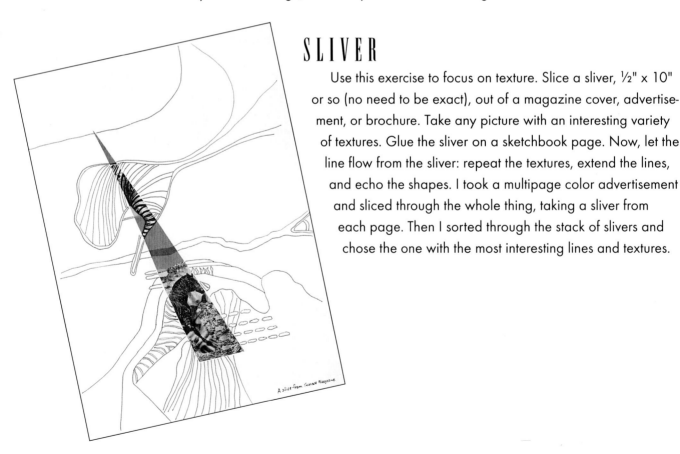

A slice from Science Magazine

SLIVER

Use this exercise to focus on texture. Slice a sliver, ½" x 10" or so (no need to be exact), out of a magazine cover, advertisement, or brochure. Take any picture with an interesting variety of textures. Glue the sliver on a sketchbook page. Now, let the line flow from the sliver: repeat the textures, extend the lines, and echo the shapes. I took a multipage color advertisement and sliced through the whole thing, taking a sliver from each page. Then I sorted through the stack of slivers and chose the one with the most interesting lines and textures.

VIEWFINDER

A viewfinder is a note card with a shape cut out of it. I place viewfinders on all sorts of images, using the cut-out window to isolate appealing compositions. To make your own viewfinder, Cut a 1½" square in the center of a 3" x 5" or 4" x 6" note card. Make several viewfinder variations by cutting odd shapes 2" across or smaller. The shape can be almost anything: a star, circle, or rectangle.

Find a book that has compelling photos or illustrations. Place your viewfinder over a picture and move it around until you have isolated an intriguing composition. Ignore color. In your sketchbook, do a line drawing of the image. I used the viewfinder technique to isolate the silhouettes on pages 22–23. Books on photography, Art Nouveau, and aquatic life were my sources.

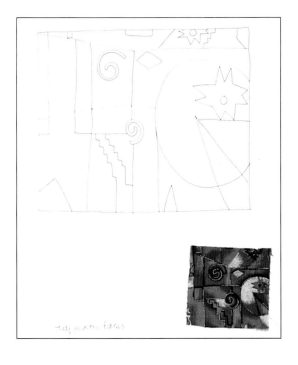

FABRIC SWATCH

As you sort through your collection of 2" or 3" squares of various print fabrics, look for squares that provide unusual mini-compositions. Choose a square and glue it into your sketchbook. Make a line drawing of the square to use as a silhouette.

NATURE

Place in your sketchbook some of the nature images you have selected. Choose an image to explore further. Work in stages. First, concentrate on shape. Draw an outline as well as you can, drawing all the shapes you can see. Turn the object, and sketch it from another angle.

Next, go back and concentrate on adding the interesting lines that represent texture. Don't worry about exactness. Try to capture a general mood.

Insects, such as the dragonfly, have captivating lines.

The fascinating texture of turkey feathers captured in a sketchbook.

Mother Nature's rocks provide interesting details upon close examination.

Last, examine the image for all the colors it holds. Identify colors one at a time, and block them onto the page. Each has an important role in the overall color composition. Pay particular attention to highlights and small changes in value. Identify every color you can. Overlap them to create the changes.

HUBCAP

The machines that surround us provide an abundance of designs. Killing time in a parking lot, I began noticing all the different hubcap designs. For the fun of it, I recorded them. The variety amazed me. These designs could easily be adapted and combined to create an interesting composition. Since the hubcap design repeats itself, I sketched partial wheels. (Draw quickly; these sketches are not intended for anyone's use but your own.) This exercise demonstrates the interesting effects you can achieve by dividing space with repeated geometric shapes.

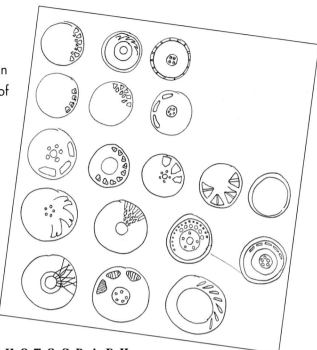

PHOTOGRAPH

Developing a line drawing from a photographic image is an excellent way to train your eye and hone your observation skills. While sorting through those vacation shots, an image may catch your eye. Choose a photograph with a peculiar angle or silhouette. Glue it into your sketchbook. Look at the picture and squint. This will help you discern highlights and value changes that divide spaces. Simplify the photo by re-creating the dominant textures and shapes in a line drawing.

FABRIC
AND TOOLS

Watching the quilting industry grow in the last few years with hundreds of innovations, libraries of books, and fabric by the truckloads confirms what I suspected: somebody out there has a bigger stash than I do. With more than 15 million quilters in the United States alone, quilting has grown into a major industry. In our small community, the quilt guild has nearly doubled in three years. Workshops that occurred twice a year now take place monthly.

There are many cotton fabrics designed just for quilters. Bolts of new fabric debut each spring and fall, outdoing the previous season's designs. I am constantly amazed by the number of unique prints, and I feel challenged to take the "woven paints" to my studio and begin a new project.

As if all the fabrics in the stores weren't enough to keep me in fabric heaven, my mother and my friends send me batiked and hand-dyed fabrics. (I know I'm spoiled.) At first, I dared not cut into these pieces; they were precious and few. I did not want to use them up. But how can I possibly experiment and explore if I'm afraid of depleting my stash? Looking at all the places to buy fabric and at their bulging shelves, I know my fear is ridiculous. And surely there is more joy from a fabric used in a quilt than from one rolled up in my basket.

COLLECTING AND EXCHANGING FABRIC

When I first began making quilts, I had very few cottons appropriate for quilting. If you have a budget (as most of us do), build slowly, buying small amounts of a wide variety of fabrics. Support your local quilt shops. They provide much more than just the latest fabrics and tools. Look for unusual hues, patterns, and contrasts. Avoid traditional calicos; select them only for unusual hues. Express yourself with large and small stripes, plaids, florals, and prints, creating an intriguing patchwork of mood.

Cottons are easiest to work with; however, consider other fabrics. There is a variety of striking decorator fabrics available. They lend themselves wonderfully to quilting, particularly drapery-weight cotton-polyester blends. Fabrics with texture, naps, and nubby weaves, such as silk, flannel, jacquard, embossed fabrics, and glazed chintz, are also fun. Visit fabric stores, taking time to walk up and down each aisle. Keep your eyes open and your mind clear of "shoulds" and "should nots" as you cruise *all* the aisles, not just the quilting cottons. If a fabric catches your eye, take a small sample home to play with.

For more variety in your collection, trade fabrics with other quilters. If they have been quilting for a couple of years, they may have huge fabric stashes. Tell your other sewing friends you have quilting fever and would love scraps from their projects.

Have your family and friends give you fabric as gifts. My brother sends me fabrics, with notes indicating his favorites. (Yes, I made him a quilt.)

Look for fabric at rummage sales or auctions. Watch the newspaper. If there are quilts or sewing items listed, you might find a fabric stash that only another quilter would appreciate.

Join a quilting club and suggest a fabric exchange. Ask members to bring stacks of 2" or 3" squares, twenty each. Take these to the exchanging table, and take out the number of squares you put in. If you bring five stacks, then exchange for five different stacks to take home. You can choose a different theme or color each month (blues in January, reds in February, and so on).

Try a circle exchange. Have members bring in a stack of twenty circles of the same size. Decide on a size range. A range of ½" to 5" in diameter ensures there will be a variety of circle sizes to choose from.

CREATING FABRIC

Growing up with a mother who dyed fabric, watching her create glorious designs with batik, increased my awareness of fabric design. I realized the creative potential in a piece of white fabric, a blank canvas on which to build color, pattern, and texture.

Other fiber artists paint, dye, and stamp fabric to create images, textures, and colors unlike any commercial fabric. These one-of-a-kind fabrics make great additions to my collection and can alter the entire mood of a design. Combined with commercial fabrics, the special hand-dyed and painted pieces create a rich, expressive palette.

Some hand-dyed fabrics can be created in a small space—a corner of the basement or garage—without many tools. See what you can do to carve out a space for fabric dyeing. Remember to read the labels and carefully follow instructions when using dyes and chemicals.

Here are some ways to design fabric. Some methods are easy and require only an adventurous spirit, but others require research or instruction. There are many books and classes available on each of these techniques. Treat yourself to these valuable resources if the passion for creating your own fabric is strong.

Batik fabric by Jeanette Sciara. Bleached and stenciled fabric by Lori Monson-Huus.

Spray paint fabric by layering it with three or more colors. Experiment by depressing the nozzle to get a heavy, spattered spray instead of a light, misty spray. Do this outside or in a well-ventilated area. Set colors with a hot iron, using a pressing cloth.

Sponge paint fabric using shapes cut from sponges. Dip the sponges into paint and press onto the cloth.

Stencil your fabric by cutting a design out of heavy paper or stencil plastic. Place the plastic on the fabric and spray or sponge paint over it. The design you cut from the stencil will appear on the fabric.

Tie dyeing involves folding and tying fabric with string or rubber bands. Dye can be brushed on, or you can dip fabric into the dye.

Stamp fabric with paint or dye to create a pattern. Use a precut stamp, or make your own.

Marbling or floating paints on a medium to transfer them to fabric creates unique and fascinating patterns.

Rubbings can produce fascinating designs. Use oil pastels and practice on paper first, then create rubbings directly on fabric. Place paper or fabric on an object with a distinctive texture or raised design. Rub gently across the paper or fabric with oil pastels.

Oil pastels are great for drawing on fabric. Experiment with fabric crayons.

Over-dye fabrics. Choose commercial fabrics that have strong contrasts, such as black and white, or prints with light backgrounds. Then dye the fabric with another color. Try painting several dye colors across the fabric in bands and watch new colors form where the bands meet.

Batik, an ancient craft, is a resist technique in which waxed areas of fabric resist dye.

Shibori is a Japanese resist technique similar to tie dye. Wring, squeeze, press, and tie or stitch fabric into a three-dimensional form to resist dye.

Silk-screen printing works well with fabric paint. Using a squeegee and a screen, press the paint through a prepared screen to create a design.

Photo printing transfers photographic images to fabric. Use commercial photocopying services, or do it yourself with a transfer medium.

ORGANIZING YOUR FABRIC

I use different storage methods for different pieces of fabric. I store large flat folds, grouped by color, in plastic crates. Pieces of ¼ yard to 1 yard I roll and stand upright in plastic baskets. I have three baskets for each color, one each for lights, mediums, and darks. I place the baskets on two shelves, a cool-colors shelf and a warm-colors shelf. I like the stimulation of having my fabrics in full view.

I cut 2" and 3" squares from each of my rolled fabrics and store them in flat boxes. I use bakery boxes that are 3" deep with a large bottom, stacking the squares so each shade is visible. Having a large selection of precut squares allows me to move quickly on a project when inspiration hits. I have two scrap baskets, one for warm colors and the other for cool. My assistant, Nancy Lewis, refers to these scraps as "the compost pile."

Organizing fabric by color in baskets and boxes allows me to quickly pull out all the values in each available hue. Storing in baskets and boxes also allows me to carry fabric to a quilt in progress to view a wide selection of color alternatives.

TOOLS

Cardboard: Cereal-box cardboard is good for circle templates. Cut circles in a variety of sizes, ranging from 1" to 10" in diameter, in ½" increments. Use them for cutting freezer-paper templates and fabric, or for marking quilting lines.

Cereal-box triangle: I use this when I need to press under a long, straight edge. Place the cardboard triangle on the fabric, fold the fabric over ¼", and iron it to get a nice, straight edge for appliqué.

Compass: I use three sizes for making circles and arcs from 2" to 5 feet. One small adjustable compass makes circles 1" to 8", one (available at quilt shops) is mounted on a 12" ruler, and one is mounted on a yardstick for large circles and arcs. If you are having difficulty getting a readable line with the compass pencil, try taping a pen to the compass. Trim away the pen line as you cut out the circle.

Cotton batting: Cotton keeps the layers of fabric from shifting during machine quilting. Cotton does not stretch or beard, and it gives the quilt a flatter look.

Cutting mat: I use a 23" x 35" mat with a grid. I also use a "mini mat," 6" x 8", for cutting small shapes. Beware of green mat rub-off when using a new mat.

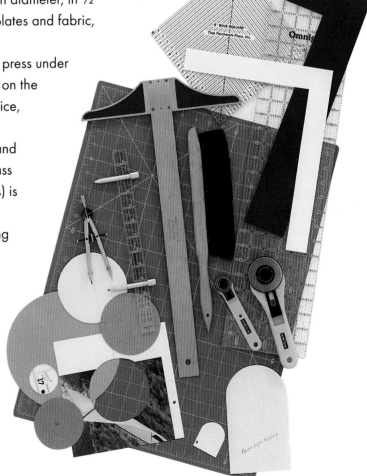

Cutting table: I use a drafting table for cutting. I can adjust the height and angle, and it has a foot rest.

Draftsman's brush: Use this soft brush to sweep off your mat after cutting, or for quick cleanup of thread clippings around the sewing machine.

Freezer paper: With freezer-paper, machine- and hand-appliquéd circles will no longer give you grief.

Iron and ironing board: I like the older irons (garage-sale finds); they are heavier, and pressing with them takes less effort. I do not use steam when pressing.

Marking tools: Experiment on a scrap first to make sure marks will erase or fade away. I use purple fade-away markers for light fabrics and silver pencils for dark fabrics. Avoid ironing over markings on fabric; the heat could set them permanently.

Masking tape: Use it to identify quilt-top sections when you are chain piecing and to "defuzz" a finished quilt. Never iron over masking tape; melted adhesive is difficult to remove.

Mat board: Cut squares of mat board, with dark and a light sides (both neutral colors), into L shapes. Place them around a completed quilt top to give you an idea of how a light or dark border would look. These L shapes can also help you square up large pieces that won't fit on your cutting board. Lay the mat board on a corner of your quilt top, mark the quilt top with an appropriate pencil or chalk, and trim it.

Needles: I use a size 80/12 needle and always begin a project with a new needle. I save my used, unbent needles for my children to use in their sewing machine, storing them in a needle holder marked "Used."

Newsprint: Use this inexpensive paper as a stabilizer for machine appliqué.

Rotary cutter: The large size easily cuts through several thicknesses of fabric. The small cutter works best for cutting large arcs and simple shapes. Always use a sharp blade, and be careful not to gouge your mat when cutting around curves.

Safety pins: I pin-baste for machine quilting, using 1" safety pins. I stick the pins through all layers, leaving the pins open. Then I go back and close them with a Popsicle stick to save my fingernails.

Scissors: Use sharp-pointed, 5" scissors to trim appliqués and clip threads after machine quilting. Use 7" scissors to cut larger pieces of fabric.

Sewing machine: You need one that can do zigzag and straight stitches and can drop its feed dogs. You also need a darning foot and a walking foot.

Spray bottle: Use this to wet fabric when ironing. To minimize water spotting, spray the back side of glazed fabrics.

T-square and acrylic rulers: Use these as cutting guides. To prevent a ruler from moving as you cut, brush a small amount of rubber cement on the underside.

Tape measure: Use this to measure your quilts for borders and binding.

CONSTRUCTION
TECHNIQUES

After I learned the basics of quiltmaking, I felt the time required by traditional techniques limited the number of designs I could complete. Discovering different sewing-machine techniques has accelerated my process, giving me more time to practice with new designs. I still hold dear the craftsmanship of the hand. The beauty of hand-stitched quilts will always leave me gasping in awe—and wondering where the quilter found the time.

I find that using the sewing machine in almost every construction phase gives me the opportunity to explore many complex designs and textures, freeing time for the hunting and gathering phase.

CONSTRUCTING THE QUILT

Refer to "Machine Appliqué" on pages 44–45 and "Finishing Techniques" on pages 53–57 for detailed instructions on appliqué and quilt finishing.

1. Create pieced panels if desired. See page 42.

2. Sew pieced panels and other background pieces together.

3. Number the appliqué pieces, working from the back to the front.

4. If you need templates, trace them from your large drawing or cut them freehand. To make tracing your drawing easier, tape it to a window.

5. Cut shapes and appliqué them to the background in numerical order, trimming excess fabric from behind each piece.

6. Make a quilting diagram. Referring to "Drawing with the Machine" on pages 47–52, plan your quilting lines on one of the silhouette copies. Do you want to complement shapes and lines in the design, or do you want contrast? Use Line Lingo on pages 27–28 for ideas.

7. Follow the quilting diagram as you stitch. Keep it close to your sewing machine for reference. Feel free to deviate from your plan as your quilting story unfolds.

8. Attach the rod pocket and apply the binding. See pages 53–57.

9. Sign and label your quilt with an inscription block. See page 57.

CHAIN PIECING PANELS

Avoid confusion by sewing with one shade of thread in the spool and a different shade in the bobbin. If your patches flip while you're chain piecing, you'll know which side is the bottom.

1. Arrange squares on a design wall or floor as desired. Mark and number the top of each row with masking tape.

2. Stack each row of squares. I overlap the stacks and place them in a shoe box to keep them organized at the sewing-machine table.

Stack rows.

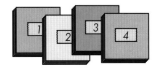

Overlap stacked rows.

3. Work with one stacked row at a time. Sew pairs of squares together in order, without lifting the presser foot between pairs. When all the squares of the first row are sewn together, cut the thread chain connecting them, restacking the pieced squares in the correct sewing order.

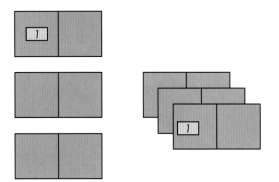

4. Sew pairs together in order until the row is complete. Stack the pairs in order

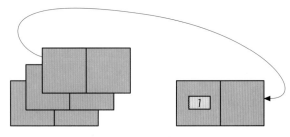

Sew pairs together.

5. Chain-piece the other stacked squares. Keep the rows in order.

Optional: Take a minute to play with the strips. Regroup them, flip, and turn them. Have fun and unlock your imagination.

6. When you've decided on a pleasing arrangement, remove the masking tape from the rows. Press the seam allowances in opposite directions from row to row so they will nest when you stitch the rows together.

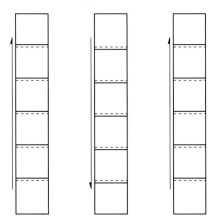

7. Stack the rows in order and stitch them together.

8. Press all seam allowances of the finished panel in the same direction. Press the back first, then the front.

STRIP PIECING ON FREEZER PAPER

This strip-piecing method is a way of adding detail in certain areas to enhance the overall design. Cut fabric strips in a full range of colors, and keep them in a cardboard box so you will have a selection at hand for strip piecing. Try building with these strips in random order. Observe the color and pattern relationships.

1. Cut a pattern of the shape to be strip pieced out of freezer paper in the finished size. Do not add seam allowances.

2. Cut fabric strips long enough to hang over the freezer paper ¼" on each side. I usually play it safe and cut strips an extra 1" in length to give me room to play with the angle of the strips. Arrange the fabric strips in whatever value or color sequence you desire.

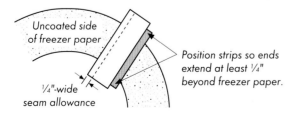

3. Place the first 2 fabric strips right sides together on the uncoated side of the freezer paper. Sew the strips together, stitching across the freezer paper.

4. Open the strips and finger-press. Align another strip with the raw edge of a previously sewn strip, and stitch across the freezer paper.

5. Continue adding strips until you have covered the paper. For a ring, add strips until the last strip overlaps the first. Fold the last strip under ¼" and use the blind-hem stitch with clear nylon thread to sew the last edge to the first piece.

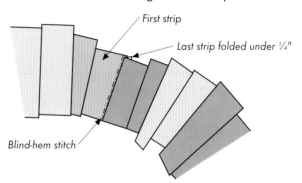

6. Trim the fabric ¼" from the edges of the freezer paper.

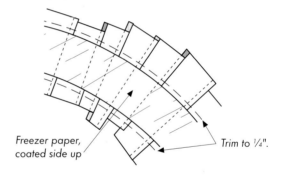

7. With a hot iron, press the ¼"-wide seam allowance to the shiny side of the freezer paper. The wax will hold the edges in place.

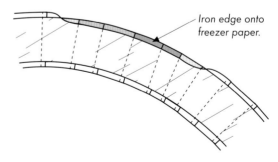

8. Appliqué the pieced section to the background fabric using the blind-hem stitch.

9. Trim away the background fabric behind the appliqué. Remove the freezer paper.

MACHINE
APPLIQUÉ

I use two machine-appliqué methods for different results: blind-hem appliqué and zigzag appliqué. With blind-hem appliqué, edges are folded under, held with freezer paper, then appliquéd using the blind-hem stitch. The blind-hem stitch is barely visible if you use clear nylon thread. This technique works well for quilts that will be washed, since there are no raw edges.

With zigzag appliqué, the edges of the appliqué pieces are not turned under. I use a zigzag stitch (not a satin stitch) with clear nylon thread. The clear thread does not define the edge of the appliqué or add another design element.

Zigzag appliqué allows me to cut intricate spirals and other free-form shapes, apply them directly to the background, and stitch with the sewing machine. Using traditional techniques to appliqué spirals would be a nightmare. Techniques and tools that accelerate the construction process free up time for you to concentrate on the design, color, and texture of your quilt. Speedy techniques can also reduce frustration, another important key to unleashing the creative spirit.

CUTTING APPLIQUÉ SHAPES

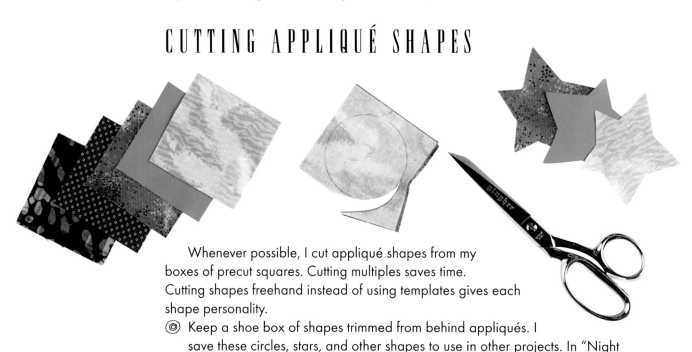

Whenever possible, I cut appliqué shapes from my boxes of precut squares. Cutting multiples saves time. Cutting shapes freehand instead of using templates gives each shape personality.

◎ Keep a shoe box of shapes trimmed from behind appliqués. I save these circles, stars, and other shapes to use in other projects. In "Night Pages" on page 71, I used many of the circle shapes cut from "Night Moons" on page 72.

◎ Cut spirals of any shape: circles, squares, or stars. Cut spirals one layer at a time, because it is too easy for multiple layers of fabric to slip. Mark the cutting line. Do not make the spiral too tight, since you will be cutting toward the center and back out again. (This actually produces two spirals at once.)

◎ If you can cut shapes using a rotary cutter, do. Small squares and triangles are easy. Layer fabrics and cut multiples to speed up the process.

◎ If you feel more comfortable working with templates for intricate shapes, draw a pattern on paper and glue it to cardboard (cereal-box weight). Cut the template from the cardboard. Store templates in a shoe box; I use my circle templates again and again.

◎ Instead of pinning, use a glue stick to hold small pieces.

BLIND-HEM APPLIQUÉ

This method works well for simple shapes, such as circles. Avoid using this method with fabrics heavier than quilting cottons, because the fabric will be difficult to fold.

1. Cut freezer-paper shapes the desired finished size. When I want to cut multiples of shapes, I fold the freezer paper in 4 layers, trace a shape on the top layer, staple the layers together, then cut out the shapes. Leave the shapes stapled until you are ready to use them.

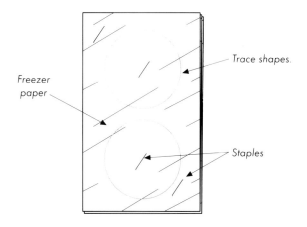

Freezer paper

Trace shapes.

Staples

2. Make a second template with ¼"-wide seam allowances for each shape, and use it to cut the shapes from fabric. A ¼"-wide seam allowance may be too wide for some small shapes.

3. Place the freezer-paper shape, shiny side up, on the wrong side of the fabric. Fold the seam allowance onto the freezer paper and press with the tip of an iron. (Be careful not to burn your fingers.) The wax on the paper holds the fabric in place. Clip curves as necessary.

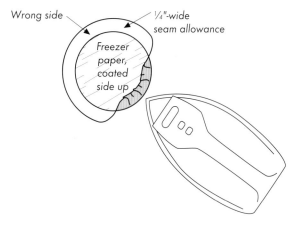

Wrong side

¼"-wide seam allowance

Freezer paper, coated side up

4. Press and pin the fabric shape to the background. Using a blind-hem stitch, stitch around the shape with clear nylon thread. Practice on a scrap first to be sure the stitch length and tension are correct. Your stitched peaks should be about ⅛" to ¼" apart. Smaller shapes will require a shorter stitch length.

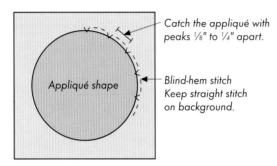

Catch the appliqué with peaks ⅛" to ¼" apart.

Appliqué shape

Blind-hem stitch Keep straight stitch on background.

5. Trim away the background fabric behind the appliqué piece, leaving a ¼"-wide seam allowance. Be careful not to slash the appliqué fabric when trimming. Remove the freezer paper. If you are working with a lightweight fabric, wait until just before you sandwich the quilt to trim the back fabric (if this does not interfere with the stitching order). This will keep the top from stretching and distorting as you handle it.

ZIGZAG APPLIQUÉ

A zigzag stitch allows you to appliqué complex shapes with ease. The smaller the shape, the shorter the stitch length you should use. Experiment on a scrap of fabric first. Try different kinds of thread: a contrasting color, a similar color, or clear or smoke-colored nylon thread. Experiment to find a look you like.

1. Cut an appliqué shape out of fabric.

2. Place the appliqué shape on the background fabric. Do not turn under the raw edges. Use a glue stick to hold the shape in place. Larger shapes can be pinned in place and the glue stick used along the edges to prevent shifting.

3. Stitch around the appliqué shape using a darning foot and a zigzag stitch. Not all darning feet are wide enough for a zigzag stitch, so check yours before beginning. Try stitching on some scraps with the feed dogs raised and lowered to see which works better for you.

Use the tip of a small scissors in your right hand to hold the appliqué fabric in position next to the darning foot. This helps move the top fabric smoothly under the presser foot. I find that with heavier fabrics, I prefer the feed dogs raised to help move the fabric through. For lightweight fabrics, lower the feed dogs to release pressure that can cause puckers. Just remember, with the feed dogs lowered, you control the stitch length and you can stitch forward and backward. This added stitching maneuverability is useful for complex shapes. You may need to loosen the tension to help prevent puckering, or use a paper stabilizer underneath the fabric. Newsprint or another lightweight paper helps, and it tears away easily.

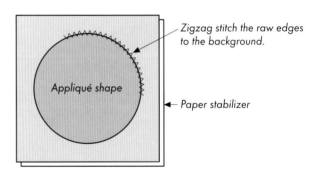

Zigzag stitch the raw edges to the background.

Appliqué shape

Paper stabilizer

4. Trim away the background fabric behind the appliqué, leaving a ¼"-wide seam allowance. Be careful not to slash the appliqué fabric.

DRAWING
WITH THE MACHINE

Quilting not only adds texture, enhancing the "close-up zone," but it is also an integral part of the design. The quilting stitch creates its own story, a layer of line that draws the viewer into the quilt. In the first stages of my quilting journey, I did not feel the need to elaborate with quilting stitches. I thought the quilting wasn't necessary, and at times I thought it even detracted from the pieced design. I was discouraged after hours of precise piecing to discover that after quilting nothing was flat and precise any more.

Have I done a turnabout now! After exposure to many quilts with beautiful, abundant stitches, I understand. The quilting stitch has a voice all its own. The conversation between the pieced design and the quilting line can be fascinating. We, the viewers, are also the listeners. What do you hear?

QUILTING DIAGRAM

Planning your quilting design with a quilting diagram will help keep you focused. Create a design, a quilt story, unique to each quilt. To make a quilting diagram, first make copies of your silhouette. With two or three copies, you will be able to experiment with more than one design.

Create several quilting diagrams, then choose the best one. The Line Lingo sheets on pages 27–28 offers many interesting textures to guide and stimulate. Post your diagram next to your sewing machine for quick reference while quilting.

Colored quilting diagram for "Heaven Help Me" by Nancy Lewis

The quilting line can be used in several ways. It can echo pieced shapes to emphasize them, flow over shapes to create contrasting texture, and create new shapes to add interesting design elements.

Quilting lines on solid fabric with a glazed finish, such as chintz, force you to take notice. Printed and textured fabrics hide the stitching. Experiment with a variety of textural effects and bold colors. Contrast thread colors with the background, or make the stitches invisible with nylon thread. An ornate quilting pattern can add excitement to a plain area. Use quilting to direct the eye toward a focal point, or try stippling for an exciting, dense texture.

THREAD

Consider all possible thread choices when deciding on color, value, and texture. Choose quality threads in a variety of thicknesses. Clear nylon thread will give you texture without a visible line. I use it in areas where I feel a hard line would be distracting. Threading clear nylon thread through a needle can be difficult. Color the end of the thread with a black marker to make the end more visible and easier to thread through the eye of the needle.

For the bobbin, I like to use neutral colors like gray, beige, or white. Usually, I purchase cone threads for the bobbin because they are more economical.

Hand-quilting thread is heavy and makes a bold, defined line. Embroidery thread is finer. Buy the best quality thread your budget can afford. Look at the entire store display of cottons, blends, rayons, metallics, polyesters, and silks. Keep an open mind about novelty threads. Ask the staff at your local quilt shops what threads they recommend. Don't be afraid to take a risk and try new threads or techniques. Someone just suggested that I try using two threads fed through the needle at once. I haven't tried it yet, but I will.

MARKING THE QUILTING PATTERN

Mark the quilt surface as little as possible. Remember to test your marker on a scrap first to determine the removability of the product. I mark small areas at a time, just before I sit down to quilt. This gives me a vivid line to follow. (Some markers fade quickly if it is humid, and pencil rubs off if handled too much between marking and quilting.)

I try to limit my marking to just a few guidelines to divide the quilt. The rest of the quilting evolves freehand within each area. This unlocks my creative door, giving me the freedom to draw with my sewing machine. I deviate from the quilting diagram as I quilt if I feel passionately that an area is calling for it. Follow your intuition.

QUILTING TIPS

◎ Beginning machine quilters might want to stay away from straight lines at first. Fluid, organic lines are much easier to sew than rigid, geometric lines. Straight lines are unforgiving and show every error, and trying to stay within a straight-line design can be extremely frustrating. Change the straight line to a curve, zigzag, or loop. The overall design will look more planned and natural, less awkward. Practice until you have confidence in your control.

◎ I usually begin stitching in the center or in the most tedious area of the quilt. I like to begin in an area that requires high concentration while I am fresh. Then I move toward the edges of the design. I take minibreaks often when I am quilting; it is easy to get tense and tired. Leave plenty of time for the quilting so you are not overwhelmed or rushed.

◎ Take the time to add enough stitching. I often spend thirty hours quilting my more intricately stitched wall hangings. I like the effect of close quilting lines. I rarely quilt lines more than 1" or 2" apart.

- If your sewing machine allows you to refill the bobbin without cutting the top thread, take advantage of it when you run out of bobbin thread in the middle of a stitching line. This makes for a smoother transition when you resume stitching.
- Relax. Don't tense your neck and back, or you will feel sore after awhile. Stay loose, and concentrate on getting the rhythm. Work with your sewing machine. Your stitch length may vary at first, but it will even up as you become more familiar with your machine's rhythm.
- Keep that first quilting project small—crib size or smaller. Larger quilts are bulky and require more skill to maneuver in the sewing machine. Pile a large quilt loosely around the machine as you work so you won't have the weight of the quilt pulling at the stitching area. This weight can cause you to struggle with the quilt and exert too much pressure, resulting in large, uneven stitches.
- Always quilt with a clean, oiled machine. Referring to your sewing machine manual, clean out the lint buildup around the feed dogs and bobbin often. Replace the needle before beginning a project to prevent skipped stitches.
- Listen to your sewing machine. When it doesn't sound right, stop and investigate. By stopping and checking at the first indication of a problem, you can usually avoid more severe problems. Ignoring the small rumblings of my sewing machine in the midnight rush to finish a quilt has left me without a machine while it was being serviced.
- Don't forget to stand back and squint from time to time. This will help you keep the overall composition in mind as you work each area. Turn the quilt over and study the back.
- Turn your quilted sandwich so you have the least amount possible rolled in the crook of the sewing-machine arm. The less fabric rolled or folded in this area, the greater the maneuverability of the sandwich.

PRACTICING WITH A DOODLE SANDWICH

Use a Doodle Sandwich to test quilting threads and perfect your stitching lines. I make a doodle piece when I want to test tension, especially important with novelty threads that require different tensions than usual. I also doodle when I am practicing a certain design line or trying to achieve a certain texture.

Practice until you become accustomed to the rhythm of the sewing machine. Do not pull at the fabric. Use a light touch and a smooth movement. Don't get discouraged if it seems difficult at first. Keep practicing; it will get easier.

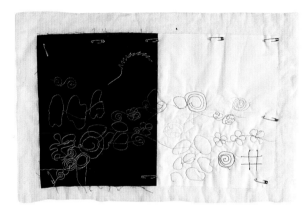

Nancy Lewis made this doodle as a practice piece before machine quilting "Heaven Help Me" on page 79, her first attempt at machine quilting. Her only problem was a few broken needles until she got the rhythm of moving the sandwich with the needle.

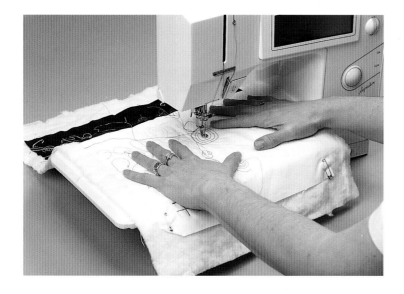

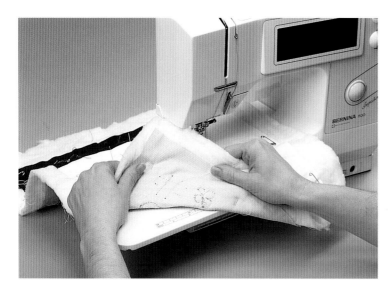

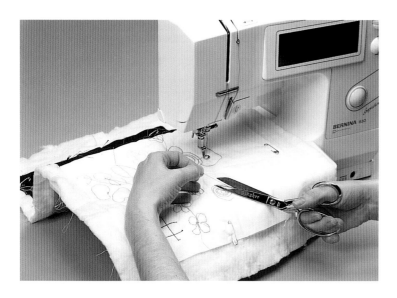

MATERIALS
Assorted threads
1 rectangle, 10" x 12", black fabric
1 rectangle, 10" x 12", white fabric
1 rectangle, 12" x 20", cotton batting
1 rectangle, 12" x 20", medium-value fabric
     for backing

DOODLING

Sew the black and white 10" x 12" rect-angles together along one 12" edge, and sandwich this top with the batting and the back-ing fabric. Pin-baste through all layers, starting at the center. Place safety pins every 6", working out from the center in a clockwise direction around the quilt. Drop the feed dogs and you are ready to quilt with a darning foot.

1. Place your hands in an L shape, with fingers slightly spread on either side of the needle. Use light pressure to hold the layers somewhat taut, but not stretched tight. Start and end the quilting line with a few small stitches, backstitch a few stitches, or take three stitches in place, one on top of the other.

2. Stitch, moving the sandwich back and forth in any direction. Stop with the needle lowered, reposition your hands and fabric, and begin again with a stitch in place to help you get your bearings. Start stitching again, slowly accelerat-ing as you go to prevent jagged lines with points where you start and stop.

3. Now practice without any marking lines. At first, just get used to the position of your hands, the movement of the sandwich, and the rhythm of the needle. Check threads on the back periodi-cally and correct the tension so the bobbin thread does not show through to the top.

4. Practice making loops without turning the sandwich, and practice stitching forward and backward. Push and pull the sandwich from side to side and back and forth. Pretend you have a blank piece of paper and the needle is your pencil. Experiment, explore, extend your mood through the needle and fabric. What kind of line would you create if you were excited or sad? Try some of the lines from the Line Lingo sheets on pages 27–28. Try building layers of line in different colors or values.

5. Stitch with the feed dogs raised and lowered to see which you like best. Remember, once you drop the feed dogs, you control the stitch length. Sometimes, when I want a little more pressure on the fabric, I leave the feed dogs up.

6. Trying different threads, stitch on the dark and the light fabrics. Watch what happens with bold and pale thread colors.

Trimming threads is easiest to do when the entire quilt, or at least a large section, is completed. Trim by pulling the thread taut, up away from the quilt surface, and clip close to the fabric. Be very careful not to snip your quilt top while trimming threads.

PREVENTING RIPPLES

◎ Start with a flat quilt top. Fix any areas that are not flat before layering with batting and backing.

◎ Use cotton batting. Cotton fibers have natural "hairy fingers" that latch onto the top and backing fabrics, minimizing shifting. Cotton fabrics also reduce shifting.

◎ Pin-baste 4" to 6" apart. Pin closer in areas that do not lie flat.

◎ Quilting lines stitched close together can reduce small areas of excess fullness.

◎ Feed fabric toward the needle evenly, without bunching in front. Position your hands in an L configuration. This acts as a hoop and keeps the layers flat.

◎ The fatter the batting, the more difficult the quilting. Use thinner batting and you will have a less bulky quilt sandwich. Experiment with doodle sandwiches, using different batting types and thicknesses to help you decide the degree of puffiness you prefer.

QUILTING "WINDMILL WASH"

I chose dark gray thread for the spool and bobbin. The back of the quilt is a light color, and the gray thread shows up dramatically.

When I first started quilting, I used only clear nylon thread. It took a bit of practice before I developed enough courage to try a high-contrast thread. I have only just begun to experiment with colored threads to achieve different effects.

I stop frequently when I am quilting to turn the quilt over and study the lines on the back. This allows me to focus on just the quilting, without the distraction of the piecing.

In my quilting diagram for "Windmill Wash" (page 62), I used wavy lines and swirling spirals to suggest a gusty wind. I echoed the arch shape with rippling lines fanning out toward the border. Soft, flowing lines contrast with the grid of squares. Ornate stitching in the plain areas of the arch draws the viewer in for a closer look.

Back of "Windmill Wash"

QUILTING "EARTH RAYS"

I chose a warm thread color that contrasted with almost every area of the quilt. The orange suggests warm solar rays.

I first divided the quilt top with a large Y-shape. I used a soft, fluid line to reflect wind and water, then went back and added detail inside and outside the Y.

I divided the remaining area into echoing appliqué shapes flowing around the silhouette. I tried to introduce a variety of contrasting lines, using the Line Lingo sheets on pages 26–27 to spark my imagination.

For me, excitement builds as the quilted textures emerge from my machine. I never really know what lines will flow from my needle as I let go and listen to the piece. Plain areas begged for quilting detail. The more lines I added, the stiffer the sandwich became. Oops, I ran out of orange thread. At 5:30 Saturday night, no fabric stores were open, and I was in the mood to sew. Since I did not want to stop, I had to find an alternative. I found a bright pink that was similar in value and intensity to the orange. Varying the color slightly added another interesting dimension to the piece.

Quilting area divided with Y-shaped line

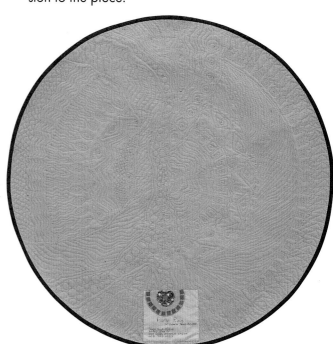

Back of "Earth Rays"

FINISHING
TECHNIQUES

ROD POCKETS

POCKET FOR A STRAIGHT-EDGE

1. Baste around the quilt top, ¼" from the raw edge, through all 3 layers. This stitching line secures the layers until you are ready to bind. Trim the batting and backing to ⅛" beyond the edge of the quilt top.

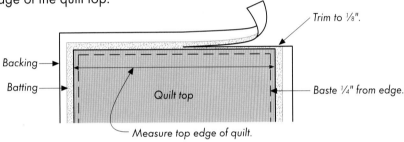

Trim to ⅛".

Backing →

Batting →

Quilt top

Baste ¼" from edge.

Measure top edge of quilt.

2. Cut a 10"-wide strip of fabric the width of the quilt minus 1½". This will be your rod pocket.

3. Turn under the short edges of the strip ¼" and hem.

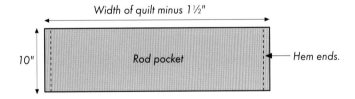

Width of quilt minus 1½"

10"

Rod pocket

Hem ends.

4. Fold the strip in half lengthwise, wrong sides together, and press.

5. Center and pin the folded strip on the back of the quilt, aligning the raw edges of the strip with the top edge of the backing. Bind the quilt. The top edges of the rod pocket will be finished inside the binding.

6. After the binding has been applied, blindstitch the folded edge of the rod pocket to the back of the quilt.

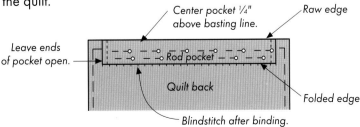

Center pocket ¼" above basting line.

Raw edge

Leave ends of pocket open.

Rod pocket

Quilt back

Folded edge

Blindstitch after binding.

POCKET FOR A CURVED EDGE

I use this method to hang circular quilts, such as "Earth Rays" on page 85, and odd-shaped quilts, such as "Inside the Morning" on page 69.

1. Baste around the quilt top, ¼" from the edge, through all 3 layers, to secure the edge until you are ready to bind. Trim the backing and batting to ⅛" beyond the quilt top edge.

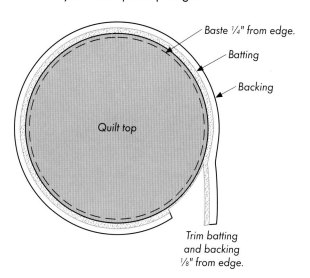

Baste ¼" from edge.

Batting

Backing

Quilt top

Trim batting and backing ⅛" from edge.

2. Cut a piece of fabric the finished width of the quilt and one-third the length of the quilt. Turn under the bottom edge ¼" and hem. Position the pocket on the quilt back and trim so the edges conform to the shape of the quilt but extend by about 1".

3. Make 2 buttonholes in the pocket fabric, 6" to 12" apart (depending on the diameter of the quilt) and 3" from the bottom edge of the pocket.

4. Pin the hemmed pocket fabric to the back of the quilt, right side out.

5. Bind the quilt. The edges of the pocket will be finished in the binding.

6. Cut ⅛"-thick hardboard to fit, and insert it into the pocket. Thread a ribbon or cord through the holes to hang your quilt.

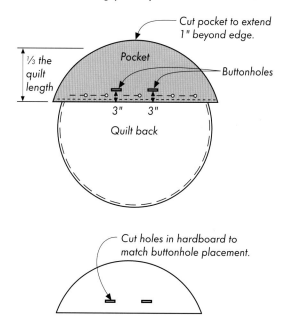

Cut pocket to extend 1" beyond edge.

⅓ the quilt length

Pocket

Buttonholes

3"   3"

Quilt back

Cut holes in hardboard to match buttonhole placement.

BINDING METHODS

FRENCH BINDING

French binding is a folded strip sewn to the front of the quilt, wrapped to the back, and hand stitched. I cut binding strips 2½" wide. I prefer to use straight-grain binding on all straight edges and bias binding on curved edges. B.O.B. (Breaking Out of the Borders) quilts, such as "Night Pages" on page 71 and "City Trees" on page 68, have unusual perimeters, so I combine straight-grain and bias binding.

1. Measure the curved edges and add 16". Cut bias strips and sew them end to end to make binding that length.

2. Measure the straight edges and add 12". Cut strips on the straight of grain and sew them together end to end to make binding that length.

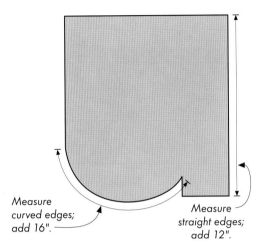

Measure curved edges; add 16".

Measure straight edges; add 12".

3. Sew the bias strips to the straight-grain strips. Fold in half and press.

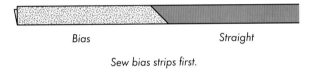

Bias

Straight

Sew bias strips first.

4. At each inside corner of the quilt, mark the intersection of the ¼"-wide seam allowances.

5. Referring to "Pocket for a Straight Edge" on page 53, pin the rod pocket to the top edge of the quilt.

6. Position the folded binding loosely around the edge of the quilt. Avoid placing seams at corners. Mark the starting point with a safety pin.

7. Sew the bias binding to the quilt, leaving a 9" tail at the beginning. Use a walking foot and thread that matches the binding.

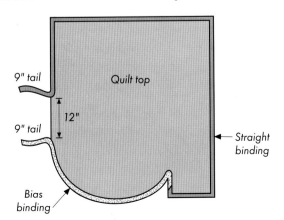

9" tail

Quilt top

9" tail

12"

Straight binding

Bias binding

8. Stop stitching exactly ¼" from the first outside corner and backstitch.

9. Turn the quilt so you will be stitching down the next edge. Fold the binding up away from the quilt, then fold it back down parallel with the edge. Begin stitching at the edge of the quilt.

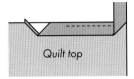

Quilt top

Quilt top

10. Continue stitching the binding to the quilt. When you reach a marked seam intersection at an inside corner, leave the needle down, pivot the quilt, and continue sewing. Clip and trim the inside corner. Practice an inside corner on scraps before attempting one on your quilt.

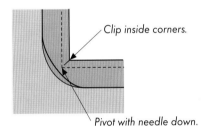

Clip inside corners.

Pivot with needle down.

11. End the stitching about 12" from the starting point. Backstitch, leaving a 9" tail.

12. Overlap the binding tails and make a clip of no more than ⅛" through the edges of the strips at the center of the unstitched edge.

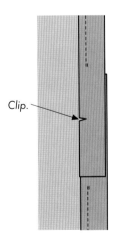

Clip.

13. Opening 1 strip at a time, mark each at the clip with a 45°-angle line. The lines should match perfectly when the open strips are overlapped. These are the stitching lines.

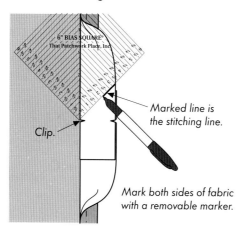

Clip.

Marked line is the stitching line.

Mark both sides of fabric with a removable marker.

14. Pin the binding strips right sides together, and sew along the stitching line. Trim to ¼" from the seam.

15. Finger-press the seam allowance to one side, refold, and finish stitching the binding to the quilt.

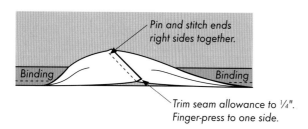

Pin and stitch ends right sides together.

Binding   Binding

Trim seam allowance to ¼". Finger-press to one side.

16. Fold the binding to the back. Pin and blindstitch in place with matching thread.

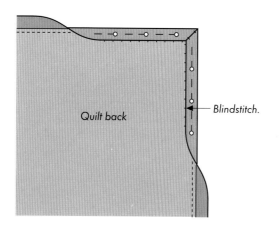

Quilt back

Blindstitch.

ZIGZAG BINDING

Use a zigzag stitch around a quilt perimeter that has many angles. I used this technique in "The Scorn of the Sky" on page 87.

1. Carefully trim the edge of the quilt after quilting, cutting through all 3 layers of the quilt sandwich.

2. Make a cardboard template of the desired edge shape, and mark the edge of the quilt using the template. (I use a fade-away marker.)

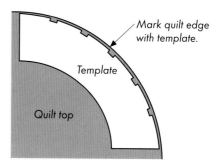

Mark quilt edge with template.

Template

Quilt top

3. Zigzag stitch with clear nylon or matching thread, following the marked line.

4. Trim close to the stitching, being careful not to cut the stitches. Now you have an unusual edge.

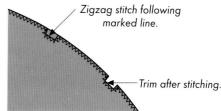

Zigzag stitch following marked line.

Trim after stitching.

COMBINATION BINDING

Use combination binding on quilts with jutting protrusions. (I call them B.O.B., or Breaking Out of the Border, quilts.)Use French binding for the straight edges, then stop where the quilt juts out and start binding again on the other side of the protrusion. For a protruding section, trim the batting and backing even with the edge of the quilt top. Retrim only the batting to $\frac{1}{16}$" from the edge, just enough so the batting isn't sneaking past the edges of the quilt top and backing. Finish the protruding section with a zigzag stitch.

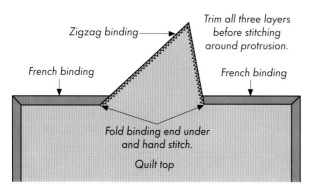

Zigzag binding

Trim all three layers before stitching around protrusion.

French binding

French binding

Fold binding end under and hand stitch.

Quilt top

AUTOGRAPHING YOUR QUILT

I like to sign and date each quilt upon completion, just as any other artist would sign their work. I sign with an ultrafine-tip permanent black marker. Practice signing on a scrap of cloth first. The ink is permanent, so take care when signing. Try different marker colors, or machine quilt or embroider your name. There are many options. Just remember to sign it. This is your unique piece of art. Be proud of it.

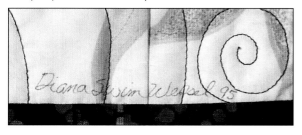

INSCRIPTION BLOCK

Make an inscription block for the back of your quilt. A 5" x 6" block is a good size for printed information and a mini-design that repeats the style and colors of the quilt top.

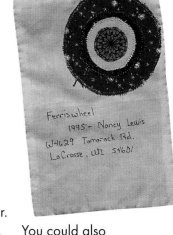

I like the block to contain the following information: name of the quilt, quilt size, year made, and the designer's name, address, and phone number.

You could also include who the quilt was made for, any special meaning the quilt has, special fabrics used, and how to care for the quilt. Embroider or use whatever method you like to print the letters. Just make it legible.

Turn under the edges of the block ¼" and pin to the back of the quilt. Hand stitch in place.

FABRIC
EXERCISES

When I first began quilting, I consciously borrowed design ideas from traditional patterns and added my own color style. Building strong roots in the past was a good start for me.

Working through these fabric exercises will help you take your beginning steps with ease. As you go, you will develop your own style and direction. Don't let your route become boring; find the edge of your comfort zone and gently push into the unfamiliar. Watch with joy as the changes in your designs emerge.

Each of the projects in this section was developed from a silhouette. Use the Silhouette Sheets on pages 22–24 to select a base design for each exercise, or create your own silhouette. Practicing on paper, I establish a silhouette and develop areas of interest by adding shapes and shading. I pull it all together with color. Then comes the fun: working with fabric (woven paints) to create a unique piece of fiber art.

FABRIC BUTTON

This exercise will familiarize you with translating color, line, and texture into fabric. Concentrate on mimicking these elements as you create a fabric button. Buttons come in a wide variety of designs and are worth observing and recording in your sketchbook. To start, choose a button with dynamic lines, shapes, and colors that would look interesting when translated into fabric. Pick up new or antique buttons from the fabric store or thrift shop, or use buttons you find at home.

Buttons are minidesigns just waiting to be turned into quilts.

Search the clearance bin and scan the hanging cards, rummaging until you find a design that excites you.

Draw the button design in your sketchbook. Concentrate on color accuracy as you draw. I like to use my colored pencils to lay in areas of color, then add another layer to get a closer representation of the hue. Take a sketchbook page and play with layering colors. You'll be surprised at your ability to mix shades and intensities with colored pencils. You'll find choosing fabrics to mimic textures easier after your sketchbook study.

Next, translate the design into fabric. Decide whether you want to represent the button exactly, or whether you want to create an interpretation of the button.

I tried two interpretations of the green button. One is strip pieced on freezer paper. The other is made of a plaid that corresponds to the button's striped background, with a padded green circle emphasizing the repeating rings in the center.

I also made the smaller, spiral-design button with different backgrounds. Which of the fabric buttons most closely resembles the actual button? Which design is most appealing?

I sprayed white paint over dark gray fabric to make the background of the large black button with the yellow outer band. Machine stitching various shades of gray on top of the sprayed area re-created the cloudlike texture of the button. Stitching before quilting adds more texture for greater interest in the close-up zone.

PANEL PLAY

The first nontraditional quilt I made was "Close to Home" (below). It was easy for me to make the leap from doing Eight Point Stars to constructing pieced panels within a grid. This was my first step toward creating something different. Now, I see the quilt is not so different from traditional designs, but it was the transition I needed to go through to get where I am now.

I made "Close to Home" for my younger brother, who wanted blacks and grays with red accents. I worked out a basic silhouette of crossed lines on graph paper, then I shaded with pencil to create dark and light areas. Blacks and whites in a checkerboard pattern provided a central focal point.

After deciding on the design and color placement, I constructed pieced panels. First, I assembled a center panel, then the arm panels with high contrast at one end, gradually transitioning to low contrast at the other end to create movement. After completing the panels, I laid them on the floor and played with their placement to test different visual effects. Working on the floor made it easy to move the panels around. I often leave panels on the floor for a couple days, checking the arrangement in different lights and various moods.

In this exercise, you translate a design into fabric using a pieced panel as a major design element. Piecing the panel from squares, you can create a checkerboard (see "Vistas" on page 66) or a wash of color from dark to light (see "Windmill Wash" on page 62, "Dark Dusk" and "Morning Open" on page 63). "I Want the Window" on page 66 contains both checkerboard and shaded panels. You can use a panel as a background to frame a focal area. You create balance and unity when you repeat the pieced panel in another part of the design.

Sometimes when I create panels, I choose a dominant hue, such as red, and work with values of that color from dark to light. Within the panel, I may introduce other hues of similar value to reflect colors used in the focal area and to balance color in the overall composition.

These contrasts keep the eye moving across the changing color scenery. Mother Nature teaches us this trick with her palette of varied hues; large blocks of uninterrupted color do not occur in our natural surroundings. A veritable feast of hues and tones blend and contrast with smaller areas of intensity.

Choose a simple silhouette from the Silhouette Sheets on pages 22–23, or create your own. Use a silhouette that is divided into a few large areas. Enlarge it to fit an 8½" x 11" piece of paper, and make a few copies.

Choose the areas of the silhouette where you want to use pieced panels. Play with value, shading from light to dark with a pencil until you know what effect you want to achieve. Roughly block in areas of color.

Select fabrics and cut them into squares. (I select from my boxes of precut squares.) Lay out squares to form a panel, following the colors and shading in your design, then sew the squares together. See "Chain Piecing Panels" on page 42.

Arrange the large panels and other pieces, then go back and add the smaller shapes from the silhouette. (See "Machine Appliqué" on pages 44–46.) Build your design, appliquéing each layer to the layer underneath.

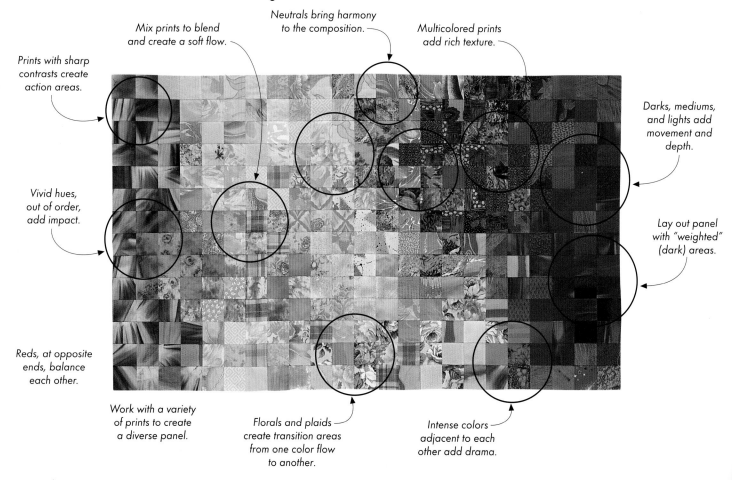

Prints with sharp contrasts create action areas.

Mix prints to blend and create a soft flow.

Neutrals bring harmony to the composition.

Multicolored prints add rich texture.

Darks, mediums, and lights add movement and depth.

Vivid hues, out of order, add impact.

Lay out panel with "weighted" (dark) areas.

Reds, at opposite ends, balance each other.

Work with a variety of prints to create a diverse panel.

Florals and plaids create transition areas from one color flow to another.

Intense colors adjacent to each other add drama.

The Never-Ending Quilt Story

I like to construct larger panels than I need, and
use the parts I trim away in another quilt.

Morning Open
Arch came from "Night Openings" (page 64).

Dark Dusk
Ring came from "Morning Open".

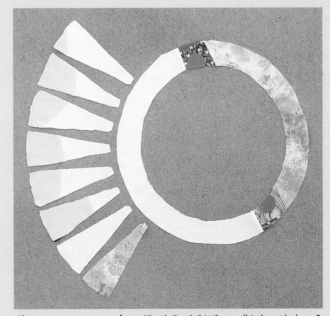

These pieces were cut from "Dark Dusk." What will I do with these?
The Never-Ending Quilt Story goes on.

WINDMILL WASH

I have an old windmill on my farm. I didn't realize that its image keeps cropping up in my work. It is a powerful symbol that goes back to my childhood. It wasn't until my windmill collapsed (the blades kind of folded up as the spokes broke) that I thought about what the windmill meant to me—security. The squeaking and whirling told me that I was home.

Inspiration

Fabric Palette

Basic Silhouette

Shaded Silhouette

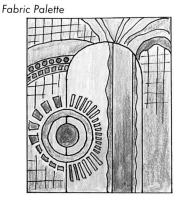

Color Added

Quilting Diagram

Quilting Detail

Inscription Block

MORNING OPEN

*by Diana Swim Wessel,
1993, West Salem,
Wisconsin, 53" x 51".
A dark arch provides a
background for the
accent fan, the focal
point of an asymmetrical
design. (Collection of
Jennifer Lief, Salem,
Oregon)*

DARK DUSK

*by Diana Swim Wessel,
1993, West Salem,
Wisconsin, 50" x 42".
A soft palette is framed
by a dark border that
flows down the sides,
creating a sense of
depth. (Collection of
Jennifer Lief, Salem,
Oregon)*

NIGHT OPENINGS

by Diana Swim Wessel, 1993, West Salem, Wisconsin, 53" x 39". Many textures of black and gray produce a rich visual story. (Collection of Allan P. and Lenore B. Sindler, San Francisco, California)

EARTH STAR

by Diana Swim Wessel, 1991, West Salem, Wisconsin, 82" in diameter. A striking Earth image floats on a sunlit background of warm hues. The planet's shadowy surface represents the destruction of our habitat.

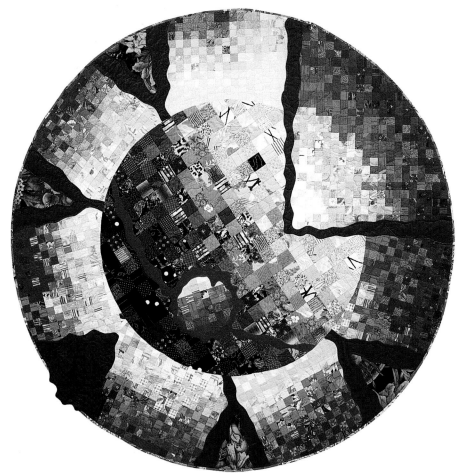

HORIZON FIRE

by Diana Swim Wessel, 1993, West Salem, Wisconsin, 70" x 80". Passionate reds, fueled by warm yellows and peaches, set afire the dark, somber night. (Collection of Sharon Strauss and Marc Schwartz, Davis, California)

I WANT THE WINDOW

by Diana Swim Wessel, 1992, West Salem, Wisconsin, 36" x 55". The checkerboard, a dynamic focal area, is surrounded by a calm blue sea. Another environmental design, this quilt was inspired by the question: "Will we wrestle for a window seat when there is no longer a view?" (Collection of Elizabeth Norton, La Crosse, Wisconsin)

VISTAS

by Diana Swim Wessel, 1992, West Salem, Wisconsin, 53" x 49". Sun colors peek through a checkerboard window, which is balanced by small patchwork openings. (Collection of Heidi and Scott Blanke, La Crosse, Wisconsin)

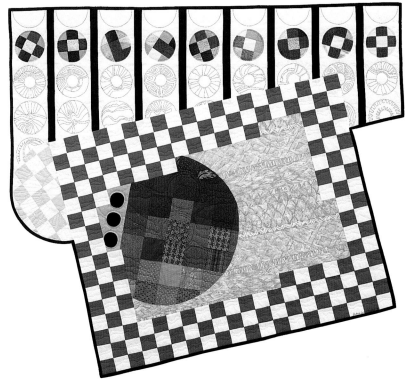

WINDOWS AT SUNRISE

by Diana Swim Wessel, 1994, West Salem, Wisconsin, 77" x 40". Sparkling jewel tones mesh to create a stunning stained-glass effect. (Collection of Cathy and Tom Edwards, La Crosse, Wisconsin)

SUNRISE WINDOWS

by Diana Swim Wessel, 1993, West Salem, Wisconsin, 51" x 38". Arched windows frame vivid and soft tones. (Collection of the University of Wisconsin at La Crosse, Alumni Museum)

CITY TREES

by Diana Swim Wessel, 1991, West Salem, Wisconsin, 56" x 83". Architectural images radiate reds and surround a landscape of city trees. This design was inspired by a concern for the environment and a fear that if we continue to devour our woodlands, our future might contain only urban trees.

MARSH MOON

by Diana Swim Wessel, 1991, West Salem, Wisconsin, 50" x 70". Grass greens, sky blues, sand beiges, and a fiery red harvest moon combine to make a marsh scene. This quilt was prompted by the destruction of wetlands and consequent loss of wildlife. (Collection of Bruce and Teresa Brenholdt, La Crosse, Wisconsin)

INSIDE THE MORNING

by Diana Swim Wessel, 1994, West Salem, Wisconsin, 56" x 45". In this summer landscape, earth tones flow along a river bank bathed in morning light. (Collection of Phyllis and Marty Olson, West Salem, Wisconsin)

PAGE PLAY

This exercise reminds me of a loose stack of pages randomly placed. On the "pages" of fabric, I placed shapes in an orderly fashion. Then I played with the arrangement, switching the positions of the pages until I found a design that pleased me.

Decide on the shapes and sizes of the fabric pages and the number you will use. For example, use all rectangles, squares, circles, or a combination of shapes.

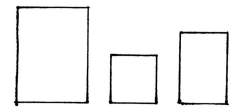

Select shapes from the Shape Sheets on pages 25–26, or from your own shape collection. Decide on the sizes of the shapes and cut templates, if needed.

Refer to the Color Composition Sheets on pages 29–30 for color schemes. Create an exciting balance of fabric textures in one of the following ways:

- ◎ Try a solid or low-key print for the background fabric, and bold hues and high-contrast prints for the shapes.
- ◎ Use loud colors and bold patterns for the background fabric, and solids or low-contrast prints for the shapes.

Choose a range of fabrics, from light to dark. Arrange these fabrics and step back to observe the effect. Is there enough or too much contrast? Cut out the pages you like.

Cut out the shapes and place them on the pages randomly or in a grid. Pin or use a glue-stick to hold them in place, then appliqué, referring to "Machine Appliqué" on pages 44–46.

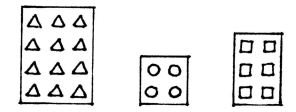

Once the individual pages are completed, then the fun begins. Experiment with different arrangements.

Appliqué the pages to the background fabric. Start with the back pages and work to the front. Trim the fabric behind each page after you appliqué.

NIGHT PAGES

For this quilt, I wanted drama. I chose pale background colors to emphasize the shapes and highlight the prints. The background—a solid, cool tone—connects the pages. The wide, dark border mimics the borders of the smaller pages. High contrast emphasizes the focal area. The pale green page protrudes beyond the border to create a dimensional effect.

Inspiration

Fabric Palette

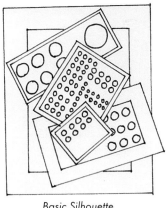

Basic Silhouette

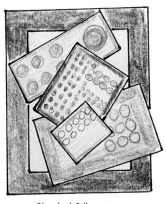

Shaded Silhouette

Color Added

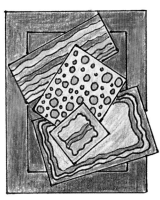

Design Variation

Quilting Diagram

Quilting Detail

Inscription Block

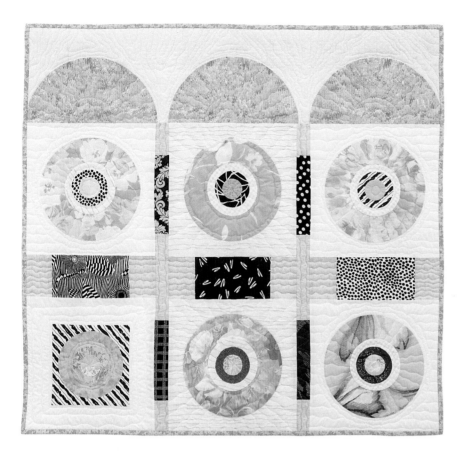

RIVER'S EDGE

by Diana Swim Wessel, 1993, West Salem, Wisconsin, 40" x 38". Layered floral pastels and black-and-white prints form sharp, dynamic images. (Collection of Marc and Cathy Swim, Tulsa, Oklahoma)

NIGHT MOONS

by Diana Swim Wessel, 1993, West Salem, Wisconsin, 44" x 44". On a bold background, layered circles of intense hues radiate energy. (Collection of Diane French Gaugush, La Crosse, Wisconsin).

GARDEN SUN

by Diana Swim Wessel, 1993, West Salem, Wisconsin, 46" x 49". Sherbet pinks and peaches bloom with pansylike images, creating a serene summer atmosphere.

SILHOUETTES

This exercise utilizes silhouettes (base designs) gathered with the aid of a viewfinder (see page 33). Locate designs in books, magazines, newspapers, and cards. Create viewfinders with unusual shapes. Using viewfinders, you can isolate silhouettes with ease.

Silhouettes can be abstracted. The maker of "Reflection" on page 78 created a landscape from a silhouette on page 22. Other silhouettes spawned space and sea scenery. "Heaven Help Me" on page 79 was a combination of silhouettes. "Space Odyssey" on page 79 reinterpreted a silhouette on page 22. Trisha, my nine-year-old daughter, searched the Silhouette Sheets and did not find one to suit her. She sat down and came up with her own silhouette and color plan for her quilt, "Starlight, Moonlight" (above right).

Select a silhouette from the Silhouette Sheets on pages 22–23, or create your own. You can use a square silhouette or any shape you like.

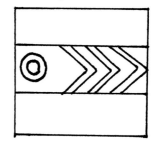

Base Design   *Flip and rotate design.*

Enlarge the silhouette to fit an 8½" x 11" page. Use a photocopy machine, enlarging the original about 200%. Make several copies of the silhouette.

Draw lines to break up the spaces within the silhouette. Sketch in some shapes. Try several compositions. Consult the Shape Sheets on pages 25–26 for ideas. Decide which shapes will enhance or echo the base design and which will add interesting detail. What mood do you want to create? What does the silhouette image say to you? Are you going to place shapes in a grid or in a random arrangement? Where is your focal point? Go back to "Design Basics" on pages 12–16 if you need ideas. Draw freehand.

Don't be concerned with your sketching accuracy—this is a working drawing, not intended for presentation. Work out a few arrangements and choose the best one. When you are satisfied with one design, make 2 or 3 copies.

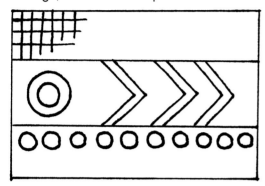

Lengthen base design. Add panel of squares. Add shapes.

Make a color plan. Don't be overly concerned with color accuracy. Roughly block in areas of color for a general idea of color placement. Think value: Where will you place dark, medium, and light areas? Think warm colors/cool colors: Which provide the look you desire? Remember that neutrals bring harmony to a design. Use intense or high-contrast colors to draw the eye toward the focal point. If you need help with your color palette, choose a swatch from the Color Composition Sheets on pages 29–30 for a preselected scheme.

Select fabrics, referring to your finalized color plan. Just one rule: No calicoes! Choose a range of fabric prints from loud to soft. Choose unusual prints with character. (I like to use a wide assortment of fabrics in one piece. "Earth Star" has more than 100 different fabrics.) Lay your fabrics next to each other. They should harmonize, work well as a group. Add a bold accent hue to build excitement. Step back and squint. Which areas blend? Which jump out? Think about color relationships as you decide on placement.

Enlarge your design to full size (the finished size you want) in one of the following ways.

◎ Draw freehand a full-size version of the silhouette. Add enough lines and shapes to show detail. If needed, use this drawing to make pattern pieces.

◎ Draw a grid on your small silhouette. Draw a grid of the same number of squares on your finished-size paper. Transfer the design lines within the small squares to the corresponding squares on your full-size drawing.

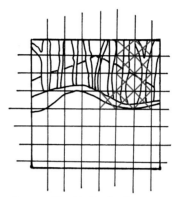

Draw a 1" grid. Mark off squares as you transfer lines to the larger grid.

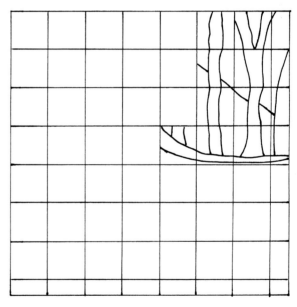

Enlarge grid. Transfer lines square by square.

◎ Use an opaque projector to project an enlarged image on a wall. Tape paper to the wall and trace the design. You can usually borrow an opaque projector from the library. (Art-supply stores and mail-order catalogs have a variety of enlargement and tracing projectors starting at about $100.)

◎ Use an overhead projector (readily available at most schools) to project an image from a transparency. Project your silhouette on the wall and trace.

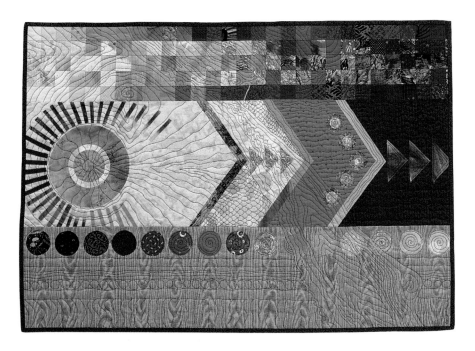

REIGN OF THE SUN

As I continue to explore quilts and design, color plays an increasingly influential role. In "Reign of the Sun," an explosion of reds demands attention. Working with powerful colors has prompted me to let color "take the wheel." With color driving, I feel I am moving into an exciting phase of my design life. Letting go of my fear of color is one of the challenges that lie ahead for me.

Inspiration

Fabric Palette

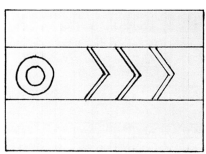

Basic Silhouette

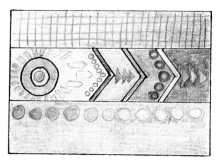

Shaded Silhouette

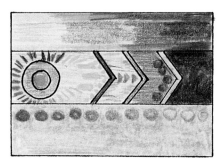

Color Added

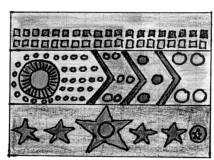

Design Variation

Quilting Design

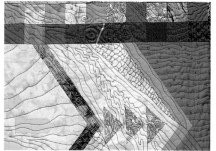

Quilting Detail

Inscription Block

COPPER COSMOS

by Joan Yeatman, 1995, La Crosse, Wisconsin, 26" x 36". Incredible marbled moonshapes stand out against bands of color.

IRIDESCENT BUBBLES

by Joan Yeatman, 1995, La Crosse, Wisconsin. Marbled moons float magnificently over pieced strips left over from another project.

REFLECTION
by Stephanie Ruetten,
1995, La Crosse,
Wisconsin, 25" x 34".
Stephanie used the
back sides of many
fabrics to make a
soft reflection with
rippling waves.

MY SEA OF
TRANQUILLITY
by Claudia DeVetter,
1995, La Crescent,
Minnesota, 24" x 24".
Cool colors and golden
sun tones create a
serene setting for this
magical mini-quilt.

HEAVEN HELP ME

by Nancy Lewis, 1995, La Crosse, Wisconsin, 50" x 30". A stimulating cosmic scene is laced with richly textured quilting.

SPACE ODYSSEY

by Carol Martinson, 1995, Onalaska, Wisconsin, 44" x 28". Lightning-bolt accents sparkle against cool blues and greens in this dramatic, appliquéd space journey.

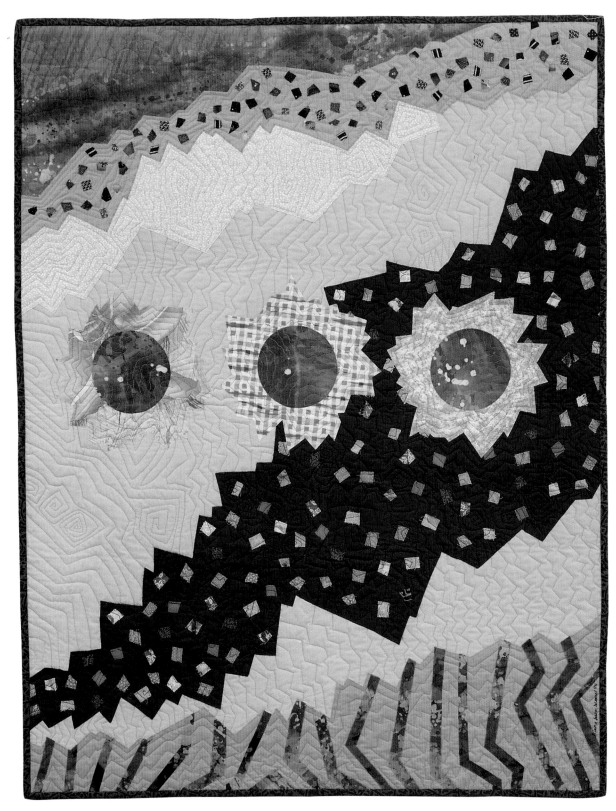

HEAT OF THE STAR
by Diana Swim Wessel, 1994, West Salem, Wisconsin, 34" x 45".
Strong contrasting hues and bold lines energize this composition.

NIGHT FIRE

*by Diana Swim Wessel,
1994, West Salem,
Wisconsin, 49" x 37".
A clear pastel back-
ground shows off
quilting stitches that
mimic the zigzag
images.*

FIRES ABOVE

*by Diana Swim Wessel,
1994, West Salem,
Wisconsin, 37" x 33".
A background of
receding cool tones is a
tranquil contrast to the
warm yellows flowing
across the quilt surface.*

MOON WINDS AND EARTH TIDES

by Diana Swim Wessel, 1994, West Salem, Wisconsin, 40" x 79". From cranberry to teal, contrasting hues awaken the eye in this stellar design. (Collection of Janet and Marc Williams, La Crosse, Wisconsin)

BULL'S-EYE

Build a medallion-style quilt, from the center out, in a bull's-eye design. This is a great way to play with color and shape in a circular format. Since your basic silhouette has already been chosen—a series of concentric rings—you can concentrate on color relationships and the interaction of shapes to create varied visual effects. You will see what I mean after you play with this circular format. Work on paper first.

Create a bull's-eye silhouette by drawing concentric circles of the desired number and sizes. Make a few 8½" x 11" copies of the silhouette.

Sketch shapes in the bands, using the Shape Sheets on pages 24–25. Make more than one design, then make copies of your favorite.

Add color to the silhouettes using colored pencils. Make two or more variations. If you get stuck, refer to the Color Composition Sheets on pages 29–30 for inspiration.

Select fabrics and group them together, making sure there are a variety of prints and a value range of light to dark. If you vary the value and intensity of the appliqué fabrics within the bands, you can create a feeling of movement. See "Night of the Moon" on page 88.

Build the bull's-eye silhouettes, beginning from the center and working outward. Appliqué the center circle to the next larger one, and trim away the fabric behind it. Appliqué the two circles to the next larger one, and trim away the fabric from the back layer. Continue building the silhouette in this manner until the bull's-eye is the desired size. You could arrange the colors from a light center to dark outer rings, or vice-versa, to create a sense of depth.

Cut the appliqué shapes and add them to the bands. I use a glue stick to hold shapes in place from the design table to the sewing machine. Trim away the fabric behind larger shapes and save the pieces for another project

As you work, step back and squint at the quilt top. Study which areas jump out and which blend. Try to identify which areas need action (loud prints or intense color) and which areas need subduing (quiet colors, tone-on-tone prints).

BULL'S-EYE SWAP

Collaborating on a project is a great way to connect with other creative spirits. It can be exciting and stimulating to see the design interpretations of another fiber artist. Sharing ideas and talents can unleash powerful artistic energy and lead to surprising results. Another benefit is that new friendships develop along with your quilts.

This bull's-eye swap is a variation of the Round Robin exchange. Instead of passing the quilt top back and forth as the design grows, each member works individually to complete a bull's-eye panel. Then group members meet to cut wedges or strips from the bull's-eyes. Divide your circles creatively.

Bull's-Eye Wedges

For the best results when you meet to begin on your bull's-eye swap project, specify the following elements:
◎ Construction techniques, such as pieced or appliquéd by machine or by hand. If you are using a machine method, decide between zigzag or blind-hem stitch. Choose a color scheme for your thread.
◎ A finished diameter measurement
◎ A color palette. Use the Color Composition Sheets on pages 29–30 for reference.

In my bull's-eye group, we chose to use machine appliqué with a zigzag stitch and monofilament thread. Our bull's-eyes were to be 36" in diameter, and we chose our color palette from a fabric swatch. Everyone in the group left with a swatch of the fabric for reference.

Swatch for Color Palette

When all the participants have completed their quilt tops, reconvene to slice the bull's-eyes. Stack the tops, matching the centers. Pin them to prevent shifting, and very carefully cut them all at once with a rotary cutter or a large, sharp pair of scissors.

Exchange slices. Each member should have one slice of her own and a slice from each of the other tops. Recombine your slices and have fun coming up with new arrangements. Your finished quilt doesn't have to look like a circle. See "The Rain Forest" on page 90.

Instead of a circle, try bull's-eye squares. Variations are endless. Experiment on paper first if you are not sure about the results. Keep seam allowances in mind.

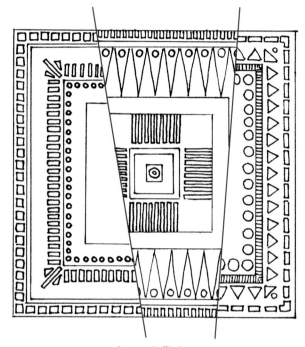

Square Bull's-Eye

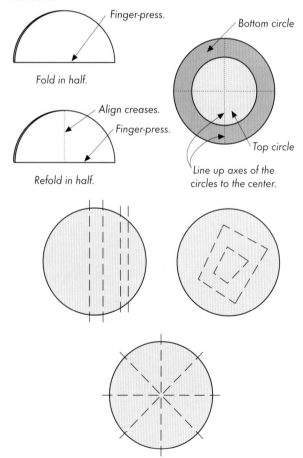

How many ways can you slice a pie?

EARTH RAYS

"Earth Rays" is a circular design, a symbol that has intrigued me for a couple of years. Maybe it is only the need to make a break from the traditional square format, but I am always drawn to designs with planetlike shapes. My seed idea for this quilt was a doily.

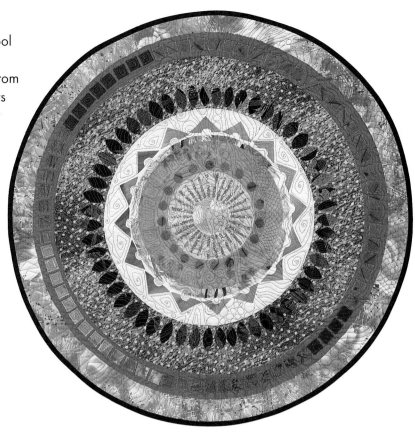

Inspiration

Fabric Palette

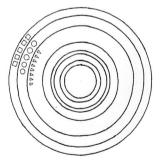

Basic Silhouette

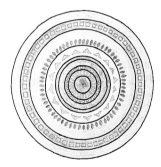

Shaded Silhouette

Color Added

Design Variation

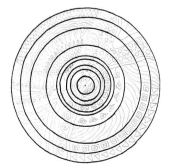

Quilting Diagram

Quilting Detail

Inscription Block

TIME WIND

*by Diana Swim Wessel, 1995, West Salem, Wisconsin, 21" in diameter. A ring of shapes
surrounds a sun image. The quilting both echoes and contrasts the shapes in the design.
(Collection of Sylvia Van Atta O'Brien, La Crosse, Wisconsin)*

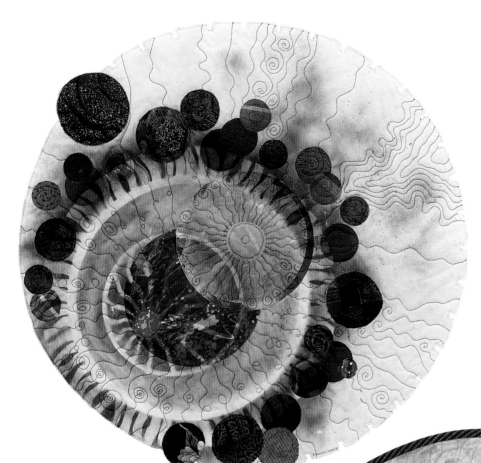

THE SCORN OF THE SKY

by Diana Swim Wessel, 1995, West Salem, Wisconsin, 31" in diameter. A shadowy, stormy image of outer space highlights a ring of planets.

WHIRLWIND

by Diana Swim Wessel, 1995, West Salem, Wisconsin, 23" in diameter. A gathering of cool sky tones and a faint layer of warm yellows surround a barely perceptible balloon image.

NIGHT OF THE MOON

by Diana Swim Wessel, 1994, West Salem, Wisconsin, 48" in diameter. A gentle warmth radiates from the central area, which is framed by night-sky blues complete with glittering constellations. (Collection of Elizabeth Doucette, Elm Grove, Wisconsin)

FERRIS WHEEL

by Nancy Lewis, 1995,
La Crosse, Wisconsin,
34" x 40". Nancy
dropped a wedge out
of the circle to make this
ferris-wheel design.

MOSAIC
BUTTERFLY

by Christine Papke,
1995, Hokah, Minne-
sota, 41" x 43".
A colorful butterfly
flutters on a passionate
purple sky.

½ SLIPPED

by Sharon Slimmen, 1995, Holmen, Wisconsin, 31" x 52". A dynamic S-shape on a black background gives Sharon's quilt movement and impact.

THE RAIN FOREST

by Nancy Reader, 1995, Onalaska, Wisconsin, 44" x 39". Nancy cut wedges into strips and reassembled them to create a compelling rainforest landscape.

FILLED WITH
FRUSTRATION?

Here are some suggestions those times when nothing seems to be going right or you've hit a road block:

◎ Take a break and leave it till tomorrow. Sometimes the "leave it till tomorrow" project lays on my studio floor for months before inspiration hits and I can get back into it. But sometimes, a couple days of mulling is all I need before the light bulb goes back on.

◎ Relieve the pressure and take a detour with mending, or try some patch play. Take out that heaping basket of scraps and have fun making patches for pants or jackets. Experiment and unlock your imagination.

◎ Make designs for tote bags. Working with bold, bright colors, create a mini-scene on a background block. Try shapes and colors you normally wouldn't use. Experiment with bright threads and zigzag around all the shapes. See what happens with the thread: it adds another design element. Sew these blocks to tote bags, pillows, or place mats.

◎ Lay out a panel of squares, even if you don't have time to sew. I often lay out a panel, then stack and place the rows in a shoe box for stitching later.

◎ Expand your mind. As I quilt in my studio, my little corner of the world, I find great satisfaction in listening to the local public radio station. This is my link to the outside world, to thought-provoking political, environmental, and spiritual issues. This radio connection is very important to my creative being.

◎ Start another project. I often have parallel projects going at the same time.

◎ Cut squares. I always seem to have a stack of just-purchased fabric. Before I roll it and put it away, I cut out a couple rows of 2" and 3" squares to add to my stash of woven paints. Sometimes viewing these new fabrics inspires me.

◎ Make stationery with blank paper and envelopes. Take a sheet of paper and create a stunning fabric border. Use a glue stick to hold the fabric on the paper. Using a darning foot, machine stitch through the fabric and paper. Try using colored threads. Making stationery is easy, and it unlocks your playfulness.

◎ Bring in another person (another family member, young or old, quilter or nonquilter) to give you a different perspective. Ask for feedback on your project. What do they see? What colors do they like? Ask for title suggestions. Many times interaction with another person will be enough to untangle my thoughts or spark an idea. It feels like fresh air fanning the fire of creativity.

◎ Stop working and view the piece upside down or sideways. Don't forget to stand back and squint. Remind yourself to keep the overall composition in mind.

If pieces are unassembled, pull them apart and rearrange them. Try six different ways if you can. It's OK to deviate from your original plan—this is where much of the excitement in design lies. Flexibility is the key. Challenge yourself to keep an open mind. My most successful pieces have that element of surprise. When I tried something different, it suddenly clicked, and wow, it worked!

SUMMING
IT UP

Let's summarize the steps to creating a successful, unique quilt design.

Observe and gather inspiration from the vast quantity of existing images, designs, and color combinations in every corner of your surroundings. Keep loose inspirations and great findings handy in a folder or scrapbook for easy reference.

Sketch, sketch, sketch. Become familiar and comfortable with pencil and paper. Designs will evolve and come together with practice.

Hunt for unusual patterns, textures, and colors that will give your quilt personality. Try creating your own fabric textures and color variations, building and adding to your collection, creating a rich and expressive palette with infinite possibilities.

Learn new techniques with your sewing machine. Practice machine quilting until you feel you are drawing with the sewing machine, using it as a tool to enhance and express the mood of the quilt.

Explore, and risk breaking the rules. Use the exercises to practice translating your ideas into fabric. Follow in my footsteps until you feel ready to strike out on your own. Then go forth, explore, experiment, and exercise your creative spirit. Take a unique fabric journey.

BIBLIOGRAPHY

Shibukawa, Ikuyoshi and Yami Takahashi. *Designer's Guide to Color*. San Francisco, California: Chronicle Books, 1984.

Sharp, Deborah T. *The Psychology of Color and Design*. Totowa, New Jersey: Littlefield Adams and Co., 1975.

Reynolds, Kimberly with Richard Seddon. *Illustrated Dictionary of Art Terms*. New York: Peter Bedrick Books, 1984.

Poulin, Berard. *The Complete Colored Pencil Book*. Cincinnati, Ohio: Northlight, 1992.

Pohribny, Arsen. *Abstract Painting*. Oxford, England: Phaidon, 1979.

Nelson, George. *How to See*. Boston, Massachusetts: Little, Brown & Company Ltd., 1977.

Kistler, Mark. *Draw Squad*. New York: Simon and Schuster, Inc., 1988.

Kennedy, Jill and Jane Varral. *Everything You Ever Wanted to Know About Fabric Painting*. London, England: B. T. Batsford Ltd., 1994.

Johnston, Ann. *Dye Painting*. Paducah, Kentucky: American Quilter's Society, 1992.

Goldsworthy, Andy. *Andy Goldsworthy: A Collaboration with Nature*. New York: Harry N. Abrams, Inc., 1990.

Frayling, Christopher, Helen Frayling, and Ron Van Der Meer. *The Art Pack*. New York: Alfred A. Knopf, Inc., 1992.

Cole, Alison. *Color*. New York: Dorling Kindersley Ltd., 1993.

Bailey, Adrian and Adrian Holloway. *The Book of Color Photography*. New York: Alfred A. Knopf, Inc., 1979.

NOTES

SELECTED TITLES FROM FIBER STUDIO PRESS AND THAT PATCHWORK PLACE

FIBER STUDIO PRESS

Complex Cloth: A Comprehensive Guide to Surface Design • Jane Dunnewold
Erika Carter: Personal Imagery in Art Quilts • Erika Carter
Inspiration Odyssey: A Journey of Self-Expression in Quilts • Diana Swim Wessel
The Nature of Design • Joan Colvin
Velda Newman: A Painter's Approach to Quilt Design • Velda Newman
    with Christine Barnes

Appliqué in Bloom • Gabrielle Swain
Bargello Quilts • Marge Edie
Blockbender Quilts • Margaret J. Miller
Colourwash Quilts • Deirdre Amsden
Freedom in Design • Mia Rozmyn
Quilted Sea Tapestries • Ginny Eckley
Watercolor Impressions • Pat Magaret & Donna Slusser
Watercolor Quilts • Pat Magaret & Donna Slusser

Many titles are available at your local quilt shop or
where fine books are sold. For more information,
write for a free color catalog to That Patchwork Place, Inc.,
PO Box 118, Bothell, WA 98041-0118 USA.

U. S. and Canada, call 1-800-426-3126 for the name
and location of the quilt shop nearest you.
Int'l: 1-206-483-3313 Fax: 1-206-486-7596
E-mail: info@patchwork.com
Web: www.patchwork.com